SKINNY SOUPS

by RUTH GLICK and NANCY BAGGETT

Surrey Books

CHICAGO

SKINNY SOUPS is published by Surrey Books, Inc.,
230 E. Ohio St., Suite 120, Chicago, IL 60611.

This book is manufactured in the U.S.A.

First edition: 10 9 8 7 6

Library of Congress Cataloging-in-Publication Data:

Glick, Ruth, 1942–
    Skinny soups / by Ruth Glick and Nancy Baggett. — 1st ed.
        210 p.   cm.
    Includes index.
    ISBN 0-940625-44-X : $19.95. — ISBN 0-940625-41-5 (pbk.) : $12.95
    1. Low-calorie diet—Recipes. 2. Soups.   I. Baggett, Nancy,
1943–   II. Title.
    RM222.2.G56   1992
    641.5'635—dc20   91-34164
                                                                    CIP

Editorial and production: *Bookcrafters, Inc., Chicago*
Nutritional analyses: *Linda R. Yoakum, M.S., R.D.*
Cover design and art direction: *Hughes & Co., Chicago*
Cover illustration: *Laurel DiGangi*
Back cover photos: *National Live Stock and Meat Board*

For free catalog and prices on quantity purchases, contact Surrey Books at
the address above.

This title is distributed to the trade by Publishers Group West.

Dedicated to . . .

Norman and Roc, who can enjoy these soups
to their hearts' content.

CONTENTS

Good Health Books from Surrey

The Free and Equal® Cookbook by Carole Kruppa
From appetizers to desserts, these 150-plus, *sugar-free* recipes will make your mouth water and your family ask for more! Make great dishes like cioppino, Caesar salad, shrimp Louisiana, stuffed peppers, and chicken cacciatore, yet keep control of calories, cholesterol, fat, and sodium. Calorie counts and diabetic exchanges.

The Free and Equal® Dessert Cookbook by Carole Kruppa
Make cheesecake, black bottom pie, chocolate bon bons, cookies, cakes—in all, 160 *sugar-free* desserts. Calorie counts and diabetic exchanges.

Skinny Soups by Ruth Glick and Nancy Baggett
More than 100 delicious, hearty, calorie-wise soups from elegant crab and mushroom bisque to exotic Malaysian chicken scallion to chilled soups and standbys such as French onion, chicken-rice, and New England fish chowder. Recipes keep careful control of fat, sodium, and cholesterol. Complete nutritional data.

The Microwave Diabetes Cookbook by Betty Marks
More than 130 delicious, time-saving, *sugar-free* recipes for everyone concerned with heart-health, and especially those with diabetes. Everything from appetizers to desserts, vichyssoise to pizza. Complete nutritional data and diabetic exchanges.

Thinner Dinners in Half the Time by Carole Kruppa
Make your own diet dishes—such as Mediterranean artichoke dip, roast pork chops Calypso, chicken Veronique, and marinated salmon with pasta—then freeze ahead to keep your fridge filled with fast fixings. You'll enjoy better taste—and better nutrition—than expensive commercial frozen foods. Over 160 delicious time-savers. Complete nutritional data.

The Restaurant Companion: A Guide to Healthier Eating Out
By Hope Warshaw, M.M.Sc., R.D.
All the practical information you need to order low-cal, low-fat, high-nutrition meals in 15 kinds of restaurants, fast-food chains, salad bars—even airlines.

Skinny Spices by Erica Levy Klein
50 nifty homemade spice blends, ranging from Ha Cha chili to Moroccan mint, to make even diet meals exciting! Spice blends require no cooking and add *zero* fat, cholesterol, or calories to food. Includes 100 recipes.

The Love Your Heart Low Cholesterol Cookbook by Carole Kruppa
Give your taste buds a treat and your heart a break with 250 low-cholesterol recipes for everything from appetizers to desserts. Enjoy the great tastes—with *no* cholesterol—of deviled eggs, Italian bean soup, oriental chicken salad, chocolate cake, and many more easy-to-make delights. Complete nutritional data.

The Love Your Heart Mediterranean Low Cholesterol Cookbook by Carole Kruppa
Lusty, hearty—sometimes exotic—dishes from southern France, Italy, Greece, Spain, and Morocco, including bouillabaisse, veal piccata, couscous, risotto, chicken Dijon, cherry clafouti, and over 190 more. Recipes, from appetizers to desserts, have been trimmed of fat, cholesterol, sodium, and calories to follow American Heart Association guidelines. Complete nutritional data with each recipe.

FOR EASIER ORDERING, CALL 1-800-326-4430

Prices include postage, insurance, and handling. Allow 4-6 weeks for delivery.

Please send: _____ **The Free and Equal® Cookbook** $12.45
_____ **The Free and Equal® Dessert Cookbook** $12.45
_____ **Skinny Soups** $15.45 (paper); $22.45 (cloth)
_____ **The Microwave Diabetes Cookbook** $13.45
_____ **Thinner Dinners in Half the Time** $13.45
_____ **The Restaurant Companion** $14.45
_____ **Skinny Spices** $11.45
_____ **The Love Your Heart Low Cholesterol Cookbook** $15.45
_____ **The Love Your Heart Mediterranean Low Cholesterol Cookbook** $15.45

Name _____ Address _____
City _____ State _____ Zip_____
Enclosed is check or money order for $_____
Amex/Visa/MasterCard no. _____ Exp. date_____
Signature (if using credit card) _____

Send Order To: Surrey Books, 230 E. Ohio St., Suite 120, Chicago, IL 60611
SATISFACTION GUARANTEED OR YOUR MONEY BACK

INTRODUCTION

S oup has always made a savory, satisfying meal, brimming with flavor and garden-fresh ingredients. In fact, soup is so popular that it has been estimated that we Americans consume 10 billion bowls a year—from grandma's chicken noodle to Manhattan clam chowder and tomato bisque. But today, there's added reason to serve more of this perennial favorite—soup can be a "super" way to help you improve your diet and maintain desired weight.

You probably know that experts are advising us to make major dietary changes. These include lowering our fat intake by eating less meat and fatty dairy products; increasing our consumption of complex carbohydrates and fiber by building meals around fresh vegetables, fruits, grains, and beans; and reaching and maintaining proper weight (weight that yo-yos continually is as unhealthful as obesity).

Happily, the recipes in this book can fit naturally into the recommended strategy. Because soups were originally devised to stretch expensive meats with more economical staples such as corn, potatoes, rice, and

1

legumes, they tend to deemphasize fatty foods and concentrate on the fiber and complex carbohydrates we should be eating more of. And they're an easy and appealing way to increase vegetable consumption, especially for those who think they're vegetable haters. Also, when carefully developed without cream and other high-fat and cholesterol ingredients and enriched with flavorful vegetables, herbs, spices, and full-bodied broths, as our recipes are, soups can be extraordinarily tempting, nutritious, *and* low in fat.

Perhaps the best—and most surprising—news is that low-fat recipes such as these can be filled with pasta, potatoes, and other filling, stick-to-the-ribs ingredients and still qualify as "skinny soups." They can be hearty enough to serve as mainstays and still play a major role in weight control or reduction regimes.

The reason is that fat is more than twice as fattening as anything else in the diet. Protein and carbohydrates have 4 calories per gram, but fats have 9 calories per gram. This means that trimming fat from recipes is a far more effective (not to mention healthier) calorie-cutting measure than reducing the amounts of so-called diet-breaking starches. To put the figures in practical terms, consider that eliminating just 3 tablespoons of oil or butter from a recipe cuts more calories than removing 2 cups of cubed potatoes or 1 cup of cooked macaroni. (And all those potatoes help you feel completely satisfied at meal's end!)

Since most experts feel that consuming less fat is *the* most important step Americans can take to improve their diet, we have made this a top priority in *Skinny Soups*. We've completely eliminated some high-cholesterol staples such as cream and butter. And a number of our light soups have virtually no fat. Many others, including numerous substantial main-dish soups, have only 2 or 3 grams of fat per serving. Some of the richest selections have 7 or 8 grams a serving, but almost all of these are kept in line with the national guidelines advising that no more than 30 percent of total calories should come from fat. (This information, plus other nutritional data, is provided at the end of each recipe.)

Fortunately, there is a very quick way to determine whether any dish, meal, or menu complies with the national guideline on fat consumption. Simply divide the total number of calories by 30; the result is always the maximum allowable grams of fat. For example, if daily intake is 2,000 calories, you divide the 2,000 by 30 to obtain the maximum grams of fat permitted, in this case about 67. For a 300-calorie serving of soup, the maximum amount of fat allowed is 10 grams since 300 divided by 30 equals 10*.

Due to our adherence to the 30 percent rule, you can eat multiple servings—or even an entire pot of soup—and still be within your fat limits for the day provided you don't exceed your recommended calorie intake.

Besides keeping fat intake low, the recipes incorporate lots of vegetables, grains, legumes, and even fruits to boost consumption of fiber, complex carbohydrates, vitamins, and minerals. They also rely mainly on herbs, spices, and other "healthy" seasonings, so less salt is needed to obtain good

*If you're wondering why dividing total calories by 30 works, the algebraic equation is:
$3/10 \times 1/9 = 3/90 = 1/30$

flavor. And these recipes are as quick and fuss-free as possible. They can be prepared by even beginning cooks and will fit comfortably into today's busy schedules.

Skinny Soups provides not only a simple, sensible way to eat right; it offers a blueprint for eating very well. Great taste and variety are key priorities so the recipes can be part of a practical, enjoyable lifetime health plan.

In browsing through the book, you'll find delectable choices for every taste, occasion, and season—from elegant sherried Crab and Mushroom Bisque and Iced Strawberry-Buttermilk Soup to spicy Mulligatawny and hearty Barbecued Beef and Vegetable Soup.

Some of our recipes, such as Split Pea with Ham and Beefy Minestrone, are slimmed-down versions of old favorites. (In the case of classics, we take particular care to make sure our "improved" versions measure up to their namesakes.) Others, such as White Bean and Angel Hair Pasta Soup and Southwest-Style Corn and Potato Chowder con Queso have been specially designed to feature savory combinations of satisfying low-fat, high-fiber ingredients. Still others—Home-Style Turkey-Vegetable Soup and Fresh Salmon Chowder with Potatoes—blend a wealth of the fiber-rich foods with flavorful broths and sensible amounts of lean meat, poultry, shellfish, or fish. There are also some tempting "creamy" soups—try Tomato Bisque, Cauliflower-Cheese Soup, and Curried Cream of Vegetable—that get their rich taste and body from careful blends of seasonings, vegetables and starches, reduced-fat cheese, milk, and pureeing techniques rather than from heavy cream.

In our own lives, we want our meals to be nourishing, healthful, varied, delicious, and relatively easy to prepare. The recipes in *Skinny Soups* satisfy these criteria for us. We hope they will for you, too.

MAKING SKINNY SOUPS

From long experience at the soupmaker's art, we've discovered some basic principles that guarantee delicious, satisfying results even in "skinny," low-fat recipes such as the ones in this book.

One obvious way we make skinny soups tempting is to rely on a wealth of fresh produce, an abundance of herbs and spices, and sensible amounts of very lean meat, poultry, and seafood. But we've also found that milder ingredients like corn, potatoes, barley, pasta, and beans are extremely useful in lending not only substance but rich, savory taste. (The starchy vegetables, grains, and beans also contribute body and "creaminess," especially if pureed in a blender until smooth.) Other valuable enhancers we sometimes call for are tomatoes, wine, lemon juice, vinegar, and the like. These heighten flavor and add welcome zest.

Savory stocks and broths have always been important in soupmaking but become essential to good flavor in calorie-conscious soups. As a result, we generally use stock, broth, or bouillon rather than water as the recipe foundation and often bolster it even more by adding soup bones during cooking.

Besides carefully building extra flavor into our soups, we have incorporated a number of important but very easy procedures to pare down fat. For example, whenever necessary, we remind you to skim fat from the soup surface at the end of the cooking period. Where appropriate, we also instruct you to choose reduced-fat products or to trim fat from meat and poultry before adding them to recipes. (The "Limiting Fat" section below includes details on low-fat sauteing, defatting canned broths, and a number of other techniques.)

Except for the simple, fat-cutting measures, however, we have kept recipes as streamlined as possible and only call for extra steps when they yield clearly superior results. If we ask you to go to the trouble of sieving a soup, for example, it's because that's the only way to obtain the velvety texture desired. If we call for soup bones as well as meat and broth in a recipe, it's because they provide a depth of flavor the recipe needs.

Also to help you enjoy cooking these soups, we've aimed to make the recipes easy to use. Instructions are clear and specific and the soups are prepared mostly with readily available ingredients. In addition, they require only everyday kitchen utensils and appliances: saucepans, large pots, wooden spoons, a blender, and a food processor. We often call for these latter two since the blender is wonderful for pureeing, and the processor is great for chopping and grating ingredients quickly.

Limiting Fat

Because eating a low-fat diet and maintaining proper weight are two major contributors to staying healthy (see the Introduction for information on national dietary guidelines), we've made limiting fat a priority in *Skinny Soups*. Following are the fat-reducing techniques employed in these recipes.

♦ *Reduced-Fat Sauteing*   In many soups flavor is enhanced by lightly sauteing the onions, garlic, and sometimes other vegetables in oil or margarine before the rest of the ingredients are added. We've found that it's possible to use far less fat for this cooking procedure than is traditionally specified: Instead of the usual 2 or 3 tablespoons, our recipes often call for 2 teaspoons or perhaps 1 tablespoon of fat, which may then be supplemented with a little stock or broth to prevent the vegetables from sticking or burning.

Skinny sauteing yields good flavor and pleasant texture, although cooking should be at a slightly lower temperature and thus may take a little longer than the conventional method.

It's also possible to "saute" fat-free by omitting the oil or margarine and using only broth or bouillon. The results of this method are not quite as savory, but it is a helpful technique if your diet restricts fat severely. Although some sources suggest sauteing vegetables using a pan sprayed with non-stick vegetable oil coating, we don't feel that it yields particularly tasty results.

♦ *Defatting Commercial Broths*   Commercial chicken and beef broth (which we often use when time is too short to prepare homemade stock) both contain fat. However, with a little advance planning they can be defatted easily. Simply store the canned broth in the refrigerator until chilled. Then remove the lid and lift off the solidified fat from the broth surface. Or, remove most of the fat from room-temperature broth by skimming the surface with a shallow spoon.

♦ *Skimming and Chilling Soups* Oil and water don't mix, which means that fat added during sauteing or released from meat and soup bones during cooking will eventually float to the top. Most of it can then be removed by skimming the surface with a large, shallow spoon at the end of the cooking period. (Don't worry if a few herbs are inadvertently removed as well; their flavor has already permeated the soup.)

Fat can be removed even more quickly and thoroughly if the soup is made a day ahead and then chilled. The layer of fat will solidify and can be neatly lifted away.

Relying on Low-Fat Ingredients

Many low-fat, low-cholesterol dairy and meat products and low-saturated fat oils are now in the markets, and to help keep our soups skinny, we have called for a number of them.

♦ *Milk and Buttermilk* While we do occasionally call for some whole milk to lend richness to creamy soups, most are made with 1% or 2% milk. And even low-fat milk is kept to the minimum needed for a rich taste. A few of our cold soups are made with buttermilk, which is a skim milk product.

♦ *Yogurt and Light Sour Cream* Low-fat or non-fat plain yogurt appears in several recipes and is an excellent way to lend zest, creamy texture, body, and high-quality protein to chilled soups. A few recipes include a sour cream garnish, and in these cases either low-fat sour cream or sour half-and-half work well (or substitute low-fat or non-fat plain yogurt if you're watching every calorie.)

♦ *Cheese* Cheese is usually a high-fat product, but by relying on reduced-fat varieties and very small quantities, we have been able to capitalize on its appealing flavor and still keep our recipes "skinny." Sometimes, we also combine it with a fat-free "cheese food product" to achieve good taste without too much fat.

♦ *Margarine* We have omitted butter due to its cholesterol, but a number of our soup recipes do include small amounts of margarine for sauteing. We always specify tub-style margarine because it's less hydrogenated than stick margarine. And we also call for "non-diet" since diet margarines tend to be watery and also burn or develop off-flavors during cooking.

♦ *Oils* In *Skinny Soups* we use only minimal amounts of low-saturated-fat vegetable oils such as canola, safflower, corn, or olive oil. Alternating among them provides a balance between polyunsaturated and monounsaturated oils. With olive oil, extra-virgin gives the most flavor per teaspoon.

♦ *Lean Meat, Poultry, and Seafood*   Meat can "beef up" flavor and add satisfying richness to a pot of soup even when used in small quantities. Since most national dietary experts recommend eating less meat and more grains, beans, and vegetables, *Skinny Soups* makes judicious use of primary protein sources (recipes usually contain no more than 2 ounces of meat per serving). Also, only the leanest cuts—such as beef round and chicken breasts—are used.

♦ *Soup Bones*   A great way to impart a meaty flavor to a pot of soup without adding lots of fat is simply to simmer bones along with the other ingredients. Pork hocks, or ham bones, and beef and poultry bones are all used frequently. While some bones, particularly ham hocks and marrow bones, exude fat during cooking, it can easily be removed afterward by skimming or chilling the soup.

Limiting Salt

In *Skinny Soups* we've lowered the salt content of soups wherever possible by seasoning with herbs and spices. However, since the recipes in the book are designed to appeal to standard American tastes, they do include salt, usually in the broth or bouillon used. (On the other hand, we usually eschew the hidden salt in such products as prepared mustard, celery salt, and garlic salt.)

Keep in mind that you also have the option of lowering the salt in recipes simply by substituting reduced-salt bouillon or broth. In addition, we provide instructions for making your own stocks (see last chapter), which are lower in sodium than their commercial counterparts. For very restricted diets, you can eliminate the salt from homemade stocks.

Also, you may want to purchase the low- or reduced-salt versions of tomato products and other canned vegetables for use in our recipes.

Using the Nutritional Analyses

A nutritional analysis follows each recipe and gives the nutritional content of an individual serving. Where there is a range of serving sizes, data has been calculated using the larger number of servings. Some recipes give you a choice of ingredients, for example, "green onions *or* regular yellow onions." The nutritional analysis is always based on the first choice *except* in the case of "beef broth, or bouillon," where the calculation is based on bouillon, which has less salt. If a recipe calls for "salt to taste," the salt has not been factored into the analysis.

When defatting is called for in a recipe, be sure not to skip this step since it has been taken into account when calculating the amount of fat per serving.

WHAT YOU NEED TO KNOW

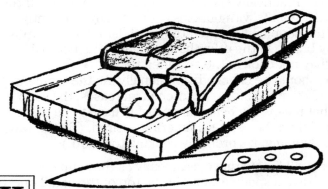

H appily, soupmaking requires mostly basic skills. Humankind, after all, has been cooking flavorful ingredients together in liquid since the dawn of civilization. And even though soupmaking has undergone a lot of culinary and nutritional refinements over time, preparing soup is still an easy, rewarding task.

Here are some tips and general information on preparing skinny soups.

Techniques and Equipment

♦ *Chopping, Dicing, and Slicing* The way vegetables and other ingredients are cut up affects not only cooking time but also the look and texture of the final dish. Moreover, the size of the cut pieces also determines

9

the volume when ingredients are measured. Therefore, we are careful to specify how this should be done in each recipe.

In the large majority of our soups containing vegetables, these are chopped. When we specify "finely chopped" we mean small pieces, roughly ⅛- to ¼-in. square. "Coarsely chopped" refers to pieces that are about ½-in. square. If directions simply say "chopped," the size should be between these two. In all cases, the pieces need not be particularly even.

Some recipes also call for "dicing." By dicing we mean cutting into small ¼-in. cubes. Here, the emphasis is on neat, even cutting.

Many soups also call for "slicing" vegetables. In this case, we often specify the thickness. However, when we simply call for "thinly sliced" ingredients, cut them about ⅛-in. thick. The food processor is not recommended for this procedure, as the slices will be paper thin. When directed to "coarsely slice," cut ingredients into approximately ¼- to ⅜-in. slices.

♦ *Reduced-Fat Sauteing*   Many of the recipes in *Skinny Soups* begin with instructions to lightly cook onions, garlic, and sometimes other vegetables in a little margarine or oil. This fat-limiting technique—which helps bring out the flavor of the ingredients—is detailed in Chapter 1.

♦ *Simmering*   You'll notice that the large majority of our recipes call for bringing the ingredients to a boil and then lowering the heat and simmering. Technically, simmering means that the mixture is cooking at about 185 to 205 degrees Fahrenheit. Practically speaking, it means the bottom of the soup should be boiling very gently, with bubbles continuously but gently breaking the surface. If the soup boils harder, too much liquid may evaporate and the bottom may burn. On the other hand, if simmer is not maintained, the ingredients may not cook in the specified time.

Long-cooking soups should be checked occasionally. As the temperature of the stove, pot, and even the air in the kitchen increases, the soup will boil more briskly. That means the heat will probably have to be turned down several times to maintain the gentle simmering desired. (By the way, if you can hear the soup bubbling, it's probably cooking too hard.)

♦ *Stirring*   Most recipes call for stirring occasionally as the soup cooks. The idea is not simply to wave a spoon around in the top of the liquid but to reach down into the pot with the utensil and redistribute the contents to prevent sticking and burning.

Stirring is even more important in recipes in which flour is added to a small amount of fat (and sometimes broth and vegetables) in a pot. Here, it's important to be sure the flour is thoroughly incorporated and then cooked slightly before any more liquid is added. Then the broth should be added gradually and the mixture stirred vigorously and continuously until it is completely smooth.

♦ *Straining and Sieving*   Directions to strain or sieve ingredients appear in a recipe only when the texture or appearance of the soup is significantly improved by taking this extra step. Occasionally, the technique is employed to quickly remove large quantities of seasoning ingredients from a stock. Sieving is not used in place of pureeing when the blender or food processor can quickly accomplish that job.

♦ **Pots and Pans**   When we don't specify pot and pan sizes by quarts, we refer to them as small, medium, and large. By this we mean:

> Small saucepan—1½ quarts or less
> Medium-sized saucepan—2 to 3 quarts
> Large saucepan—4 or more quarts
> Dutch oven or small pot—4 to 5 quarts
> Large pot—6 to 7 quarts
> Very large pot—8 quarts or larger

♦ **Blenders and Food Processors**   Blenders and food processors are two of the most useful tools in making soups. The blender is very convenient for pureeing ingredients when a smooth texture is desired. However, particular care must be taken when blending mixtures that have just been cooked. Always cool them slightly first, and start the blending process on *low speed* until the mixture is partially pureed. Then raise the speed to medium or high. As an added precaution, do not fill the container more than about half full. And cover the top of the blender container with a dish towel or cloth and hold the lid down firmly.

The food processor can also be used to puree some soups, but it is not as efficient at this task. Pureeing will take considerably longer, and the mixture will probably not be quite as smooth. Keep this in mind where recipes offer a choice of these appliances. On the other hand, the food processor chops uncooked ingredients quickly and is excellent for shredding and grating vegetables and cheese.

Ingredients

Throughout *Skinny Soups* we've tried to be as specific as possible about what ingredients to use. Following are some additional comments that may answer questions that come up.

♦ **Stock, Broth, and Bouillon**   Of necessity, cooks used to make their own soup *stock* by simmering bones and vegetables with water and seasonings in a large pot for hours. The advantage of using homemade stocks is that they need relatively small amounts of salt for full-bodied flavor. You will find several recipes for homemade stocks at the end of this book.

On the other hand, you can substitute commercial *broth* or *bouillon* for stock. Chicken or beef broth is a canned product available in liquid form. When we refer to bouillon, we mean the cubes or granules that are reconstituted with water.

Substitutes for vegetable stock include bouillon powders, granules, pastes, and cubes. The powders, sold by such manufacturers as MBT, are available in supermarkets. Health food stores sell vegetable bouillon cubes, pastes, and granules. Often these have a lower salt content than the supermarket offerings or are salt-free.

♦ *Clam Juice* This is a commercial product usually found in the canned and bottled juice department of supermarkets. In some of our fish and sea-food soups we use it as a ready-made stock.

♦ *Dried Beans* When a recipe calls for cooked beans, these are dried beans that have been cooked in unsalted water. For convenience, these can be prepared well in advance and frozen in measured quantities for later use. Do not store cooked beans in the refrigerator longer than 2 days. Canned beans, which have similar nutritive value, can be substituted in all recipes. However, canned beans are salty and will significantly increase the sodium content of soups. Rinse and drain canned beans thoroughly to remove as much salt as possible before using.

♦ *Leeks* Many American cooks are just becoming familiar with this mild, pleasant-tasting member of the onion family. However, leeks add wonderful flavor to soups. If there's a choice, avoid very large, dry looking leeks, as they may be tough.

♦ *Olive Oil* The rich, fruity taste of extra-virgin olive oil contributes significantly to the flavor of some soups. While it's not necessary to buy the most expensive brands or grades, don't pick the least expensive ones either, as these have very little flavor.

♦ *Onions* These are a mainstay of soupmaking. Unless some particular type is specified, use standard yellow cooking onions.

♦ *Parsley* Dry parsley is never suggested as a substitute for fresh in this book. When dried, parsley loses its flavor and thus contributes nothing except a little color to a recipe. If only a small amount of parsley is called for and you don't have fresh, simply omit it.

♦ *Potatoes* Potatoes can be a very important ingredient in soupmaking. They not only flavor soups but also help thicken broths. Sometimes we specifically call for "new" or "boiling potatoes," thin-skinned or brown rounded potatoes with firm, waxy flesh. If these are unavailable, choose "all purpose" potatoes over "baking potatoes."

♦ *Tomatoes* Some recipes that would otherwise be high in sodium call for reduced-sodium tomatoes, tomato sauce, or stewed tomatoes. You can, of course, substitute regular canned tomato sauce or stewed tomatoes if you're not overly concerned about sodium in your diet. Also, in cases where a full-bodied tomato flavor is essential, we call for Italian (plum) tomatoes or Italian-style tomatoes.

♦ *Wine* Unless a specific type is called for, any pleasant, inexpensive table wine can be used. Do not substitute "cooking wine" of the sort sold in supermarkets. It is usually much too salty and often too strong and sour as well. Similarly, in recipes that specify "sherry," use an inexpensive dry or medium-dry sherry; "cooking sherry" is not satisfactory. Unlike other wine, sherry keeps well for several months at room temperature after it has been opened.

VEGETABLE SOUPS

CELERY-TOMATO SOUP

Although quick and easy, this recipe showcases the delicate flavor and crisp texture of a vegetable that is usually assigned a supporting rather than primary role in soup cookery. The soup also tastes good served cold.

Makes 6 to 8 Servings.

- 1 tablespoon non-diet, tub-style margarine
- 4 cups celery, thinly sliced
- 2 medium-sized onions, finely chopped
- 3 cups chicken broth (defatted), divided
- ¼ cup fresh parsley leaves, finely chopped

½ cup dry white wine, *or* dry sherry
1 teaspoon dried marjoram leaves
¼ teaspoon (generous) dried thyme leaves
¼ teaspoon dried tarragon leaves
⅛ teaspoon black pepper
2 16-oz. cans tomatoes, including juice, pureed in blender or food processor
1 teaspoon sugar
Salt to taste

I n a large saucepan or Dutch oven, melt margarine over medium heat. Add celery and onion and 3 tablespoons chicken broth and cook, stirring frequently, 6 or 7 minutes until onion is soft. If liquid begins to evaporate, add a bit more broth.

Add remaining chicken broth, parsley, white wine, marjoram, thyme, tarragon, and black pepper. Bring to boil, then cover, lower heat, and simmer, stirring occasionally, about 20 minutes or until celery is just tender.

Add tomatoes, sugar, and salt (if desired) and stir to combine well. Simmer, covered, an additional 5 minutes.

This soup keeps 3 to 4 days in refrigerator.

Number of Servings: 8 (data per serving)

calories:	78	protein:	3.7
% calories from fat:	23	fat: (gm):	2.0
cholesterol (mg):	0	sodium (mg):	427

HERBED BROCCOLI-CAULIFLOWER BISQUE

◆

Makes 5 to 6 Servings.

2 medium broccoli stalks
½ small head of cauliflower
2 teaspoons non-diet, tub-style margarine
1 cup green onions, chopped
1 tablespoon all-purpose white flour
3 cups chicken stock, *or* broth (defatted)
1⅓ cups boiling potatoes, peeled and coarsely chopped
⅛ teaspoon (generous) black pepper
3 tablespoons fresh chives, finely chopped or 1½ tablespoons dried chives
2½ teaspoons dried basil leaves
1½ cups 2% milk
Salt to taste

C ut enough small, tender tops from broccoli florets to yield ¾ cup of ¼-in. floret tips. Reserve. Repeat process with cauliflower, reserving ¾ cup tender ¼-in. floret tips. Coarsely chop enough more florets and tender stem pieces from broccoli to yield 1 cup. Repeat process with cauliflower, coarsely chopping enough florets and tender stems to yield ⅔ cup.

In a medium pot, combine margarine and onions. Cook over medium heat, stirring frequently, until onions are limp, about 4 minutes. Stir in flour until incorporated. Cook, stirring, 30 seconds. Gradually stir in stock until incorporated smoothly into flour. Stir in chopped broccoli and cauliflower (reserve floret tips for adding later). Add potatoes, pepper, chives, and basil.

Bring mixture to a boil over medium-high heat. Lower heat and simmer, uncovered and stirring occasionally, 12 to 14 minutes or until potatoes are tender.

In two batches, puree cooked vegetable-broth mixture in blender until completely pureed and smooth. Return puree, milk, and reserved broccoli and cauliflower floret tips to pot. Let mixture return to a simmer, and simmer 3 to 5 minutes longer, until floret tips are just cooked through but still slightly crisp. Add salt if desired. Serve immediately.

Bisque may be stored in refrigerator up to 2 days.

Number of Servings: 6 *(data per serving)*

calories:	97	protein (mg):	6.5
% calories from fat:	26	fat (gm):	2.8
cholesterol (mg):	5	sodium (mg):	273

CREAMY BROCCOLI-POTATO SOUP

Broccoli-Potato Soup can also be served cold as a Broccoli Vichyssoise. To serve cold, stir in 1 tablespoon of lemon juice, ¼ cup additional chicken stock, and (if sodium is no concern) increase the salt slightly to taste. Then chill about 5 hours. Garnish individual servings with lemon slices.

Makes 6 to 8 Servings.

- 4 medium-sized leeks (about 1 lb.)
- 2 teaspoons non-diet, tub-style margarine
- 3 cups chicken stock, *or* broth (defatted), divided
- 1½ lbs. boiling potatoes, peeled and diced (3½ cups diced potatoes)
- 4 cups broccoli florets
- ¼ teaspoon white pepper
- 1¼ cups whole milk
  Salt to taste
- 1 to 2 teaspoons finely chopped chives for garnish (optional)

Since sand and dirt collect under the leaves of leeks, clean them very carefully as follows: Trim off and discard root end and all but about 1 in. of the green tops. Peel off and discard 1 or 2 layers of tough outer leaves. Then, beginning at the green end, slice down about 1 in. into leeks. Put leeks into colander. Wash them thoroughly under cool running water; wash again to remove all traces of dirt. Set them aside until well drained. Cut leeks crosswise into ½-in. pieces.

In Dutch oven or very large saucepan, melt margarine over medium heat. Add leeks and 3 tablespoons of stock and cook, stirring frequently, about 10 minutes until leeks are tender but not browned. If liquid begins to evaporate, lower heat slightly and add more stock. Add remaining chicken stock, potatoes, broccoli, and pepper.

Lower heat, cover, and simmer about 11 to 14 minutes or until potatoes and broccoli are tender. Remove pot from heat and let cool slightly. In batches, puree mixture in a blender on low speed for 10 seconds. Then raise speed to high and puree until completely smooth. Return puree to pot in which it was cooked. Add milk and stir to mix well. Simmer an additional 4 to 5 minutes. Add salt if desired.

Serve in medium-sized bowls. Garnish individual servings with sprinkling of chopped chives if desired.

This soup keeps 2 to 3 days in refrigerator.

Number of Servings: 8 *(data per serving)*

calories:	163	protein (gm):	6.7
% calories from fat:	15	fat (gm):	2.8
cholesterol (mg):	5	sodium (mg):	219

CREOLE TOMATO SOUP

Tomatoes, green pepper, and spices combine to give this soup a Creole flavor. A nice, quick alternative to vegetable soup, it can be served as a first course or as part of a soup-and-sandwich meal.

Makes 4 Servings.

2 teaspoons non-diet tub-style margarine
1 medium-sized sweet green pepper, diced
1 medium-sized onion, finely chopped
1 medium-sized garlic clove, minced
2 cups chicken or vegetable bouillon, reconstituted from cubes or granules, divided
2 16-oz. cans tomatoes, including juice, pureed in a blender or food processor
2 teaspoons sugar
1 teaspoon (scant) dried marjoram leaves
½ teaspoon dried basil leaves
¼ teaspoon dried thyme leaves
2 bay leaves
Dash cayenne pepper
¼ teaspoon black pepper
Salt to taste

I n a Dutch oven over medium heat, melt margarine. Add green pepper, onion, garlic, and 3 tablespoons bouillon. Cook, stirring, about 4 to 5 minutes until onion is soft. If liquid begins to evaporate, add a bit more bouillon.

Add all remaining ingredients except salt. Cover and bring to a boil. Lower heat and simmer soup about 15 minutes or until green pepper is tender and flavors are well blended. Add salt if desired.

This soup keeps 2 to 3 days in refrigerator.

Number of Servings: 4 *(data per serving)*

calories: 87		protein (gm):	3.0
% calories from fat:	28	fat (gm):	2.7
cholesterol (mg):	0	sodium (mg):	827

LENTIL-VEGETABLE SOUP

Because red lentils cook quickly, you can have this soup on the table in less than 35 minutes. The lentils and rice combine to make a complete protein.

Makes 6 Servings.

- 1 large onion, finely chopped
- 1 large celery stalk, diced
- 1 large garlic clove, minced
- 1 teaspoon olive oil
- 2 cups chicken bouillon, reconstituted from cubes
- 1 large carrot, diced
- 1 16-oz. can reduced-sodium stewed tomatoes, *or* regular stewed tomatoes
- ⅓ cup red lentils, rinsed and sorted
- 2 cups water
- ½ large green pepper, diced
- 1½ cups small zucchini cubes
- 3 tablespoons long-grain white rice
- ½ teaspoon dried thyme leaves
- 1 bay leaf
- ½ teaspoon dried basil leaves
- ½ teaspoon sugar
- ¼ teaspoon ground cumin
- ⅛ teaspoon black pepper
  Salt to taste

In a Dutch oven or large, heavy pot, combine onion, celery, garlic, olive oil, and 3 tablespoons bouillon. Cook over medium heat, stirring frequently, until onion is tender. Add all remaining ingredients except salt. Bring to a boil. Lower heat and simmer 25 minutes or until lentils are tender. Add salt if desired.

Number of Servings: 6 *(data per serving)*

calories:	91	protein (gm):	4.0
% calories from fat:	12	fat (gm):	1.2
cholesterol (mg):	0	sodium (mg):	317

POTATO-KALE SOUP

Fresh kale adds a subtle and pleasing flavor to this creamy soup, which is based on a traditional Irish recipe.

Makes 5 to 6 Servings.

2 teaspoons non-diet, tub-style margarine
1 very large garlic clove, minced
2 medium-sized onions, finely chopped
4 beef bouillon cubes reconstituted with 3 cups water, divided
4½ cups potatoes, peeled and cut into ¾-in. cubes (about 1⅜ lbs.)
2 cups whole milk
½ teaspoon dried thyme leaves
¼ teaspoon dry mustard
⅛ teaspoon ground celery seed
6 cups tender kale leaves, mid-ribs removed, and coarsely chopped
¼ teaspoon (scant) black pepper
Salt to taste

I n a Dutch oven or soup pot, combine margarine, garlic, onion, and 3 tablespoons bouillon. Cook, stirring frequently, over medium heat 6 or 7 minutes until onion is tender. If liquid begins to evaporate, add a bit more bouillon.

Add potatoes, remaining beef bouillon, milk, thyme, dry mustard, and ground celery seed. Bring to a boil. Cover, reduce heat, and simmer about 15 minutes or until potatoes are very tender. Remove pot from heat.

In a food processor or blender, in batches if necessary, puree about half of the milk-potato mixture and return it to pot. Return pot to heat. Add kale and pepper. Bring soup to a boil and reduce heat. Simmer an additional 12 to 15 minutes, stirring occasionally, until kale is just tender. Taste soup. Add salt if desired. Stir before serving.

This soup keeps well in refrigerator 1 or 2 days if young, tender kale has been used. Older kale will change flavor of the soup after refrigeration.

Number of Servings: 6 *(data per serving)*

calories:	189	protein (gm):	6.6
% calories from fat:	22	fat (gm):	4.6
cholesterol (mg):	11	sodium (mg):	654

CAULIFLOWER CHEESE SOUP

If you love the taste of cheese, you'll appreciate the rich flavor of this soup, which combines a very small amount of real Cheddar with non-fat Cheddar cheese food.

Makes 4 to 5 Servings.

1 small onion, finely chopped
1 small clove garlic, chopped
3 cups chicken broth or stock (defatted), divided
1⅓ cups potatoes, peeled and diced
2 cups small cauliflower pieces, including stems
¼ teaspoon dry mustard powder
⅛ teaspoon ground celery seed
⅛ teaspoon white pepper, or to taste
¾ cup 1% milk
½ cup grated or shredded Alpine Lace non-fat Cheddar cheese food (about 2 ozs.)
½ cup shredded Cheddar cheese (about 1½ ozs.)
Chopped chives for garnish

In a medium-sized pot, combine onion, garlic, and 3 tablespoons of stock. Cook, stirring occasionally, 4 or 5 minutes or until onion is soft. If liquid begins to evaporate, add a bit more stock. Add remainder of stock, potatoes, cauliflower, mustard powder, ground celery seed, and white pepper.

Bring to a boil over high heat. Lower heat, cover, and simmer 11 to 14 minutes until potatoes and cauliflower are tender. Remove pot from heat.

In batches, puree a generous three-quarters of the vegetables and liquid in blender. Return puree to pot with remaining vegetables and liquid. Add milk and stir to mix well.

Heat soup to a gentle simmer. Add non-fat cheese food to soup, stirring well. Add the shredded Cheddar cheese and stir until it melts. (The non-fat cheese food will not melt completely.) Cook an additional minute or two, but *do not boil.* Garnish each serving with chives.

This soup keeps in refrigerator 1 to 2 days.

Number of Servings: 5 *(data per serving)*

calories:	142	protein (gm):	11.8
% calories from fat:	29	fat (gm):	4.5
cholesterol (mg):	14	sodium (mg):	512

SESAME NOODLE SOUP

◆

Light, tasty, and full of contrasting textures, this oriental noodle soup is great for lunch. We specify Shoyu brand light soy sauce because it has only 80 milligrams of sodium per ½ teaspoon. Other brands of light soy sauce could be used, but they have more sodium.

◆

Makes 5 to 6 Servings.

1 teaspoon sesame oil
1 teaspoon fresh ginger, minced
1 garlic clove, minced
½ cup scallions, including green tops, thinly sliced
3 cups bok choy (Chinese cabbage) stems and green leaves, thinly sliced
5 cups chicken broth (defatted), divided
1 cup water
1 tablespoon Shoyu light (reduced-salt) soy sauce (or more if desired)
4 ozs. thin spaghetti, broken into 2-in. pieces (about 2 cups)
1 8-oz. can sliced water chestnuts, drained
5 ozs. fresh tofu cut into ½-in. cubes (about ⅔ cup)

Combine sesame oil, ginger, garlic, scallions, bok choy, and 3 table-spoons chicken broth in large saucepan or Dutch oven over medium heat. Cook, stirring frequently, about 3 minutes or until onion is almost tender.

Add remaining broth, water, and soy sauce. Bring soup to a boil. Add spaghetti, reduce heat, and cook, covered, about 8 minutes or until spaghetti is almost tender. Add water chestnuts and tofu. Bring to a boil again and cook an additional 2 minutes until tofu is cooked and flavors are blended.

◆

Number of Servings: 6 *(data per serving)*

calories:	202	protein (gm):	11.8
% calories from fat:	12	fat (gm):	2.8
cholesterol (mg):	1	sodium (mg):	536

CREAMY TOMATO SOUP WITH CHUNKY VEGETABLES

Makes 5 to 6 Servings.

- 2 teaspoons non-diet, tub-style margarine
- 1 medium-sized onion, finely chopped
- 1 large garlic clove, minced
- 3 cups chicken stock or broth (defatted), divided
- 1 large celery stalk, diced
- 1½ cups unpeeled new potatoes cut into ¾-in. cubes (2 small potatoes)
- 1½ cups 1-in. cauliflower pieces
- 1 cup zucchini, diced
- 1 medium-sized sweet green pepper, diced
- ¼ cup dry sherry
- ¼ cup fresh parsley leaves, finely chopped
- ¾ teaspoon dried basil leaves
- ¼ teaspoon (generous) dried thyme leaves
- ¼ teaspoon (generous) dried marjoram leaves
- ⅛ teaspoon powdered mustard
  Dash cayenne pepper
- ⅛ teaspoon black pepper
- 1½ tablespoons cornstarch
- ¼ cup cold water
- 1 8-oz. can tomato sauce
- ¾ cup whole milk
  Salt to taste

I n a large saucepan or small pot, melt margarine over medium heat. Add onion and garlic and 2 tablespoons of stock. Cook, stirring frequently, until onion is soft, about 5 minutes. If onion begins to stick to pot, add a bit more stock.

Add remaining stock, celery, potatoes, cauliflower, zucchini, green pepper, sherry, parsley, basil, thyme, marjoram, mustard, cayenne pepper, and black pepper. Bring mixture to a boil. Cover, lower heat, and simmer about 15 to 20 minutes or until vegetables are tender. (The celery will be crisp-tender.)

Meanwhile, in a small bowl, stir cornstarch and water together until thoroughly blended. Add cornstarch-water mixture to liquid in the pot.

Raise heat slightly and cook, stirring frequently, until stock thickens and boils, about 1 to 2 minutes.

Lower heat again. Stir in tomato sauce, milk, and salt if desired. Heat soup an additional 4 or 5 minutes.

This soup keeps 2 to 3 days in refrigerator.

Number of Servings: 6 *(data per serving)*

calories:	137	protein (gm):	6.0
% calories from fat:	18	fat (gm):	2.8
cholesterol (mg):	4	sodium (mg):	506

PUMPKIN SOUP

◆

Although most people have only tasted pumpkin in pies and other baked goods, it also makes a tasty soup.

◆

Makes 4 to 5 Servings.

2	teaspoons non-diet, tub-style margarine
1	medium-sized onion, finely chopped
2	celery stalks, finely chopped
1	medium-sized carrot, finely chopped
2½	cups chicken broth (defatted), divided
2	tablespoons all-purpose white flour
1½	cups canned pumpkin puree (not pie filling)
1	cup 1% milk
2	teaspoons sugar
⅛	teaspoon ground ginger
⅛	teaspoon ground nutmeg
⅛	teaspoon ground cloves
⅛	teaspoon ground mace
⅛	teaspoon white pepper
	Salt to taste

I n a large saucepan, melt margarine over medium heat. Add onion, celery, carrot, and 3 tablespoons of broth. Cook, stirring frequently, 5 or 6 minutes or until onion is soft. If liquid begins to evaporate, add a bit more broth. Remove pot from heat.

Add flour to the vegetable mixture and stir to combine well. Return pot to heat. Cook, stirring, for 1 minute. Slowly add remaining stock, stirring so that no lumps form. Stir in pumpkin, milk, sugar, spices, and salt (if desired). Bring to a boil. Lower heat and simmer, covered, about 20 minutes or until vegetables are tender.

This soup keeps 1 to 2 days in the refrigerator.

◆

Number of Servings: 5 *(data per serving)*

calories:	108	protein (gm):	5.7
% calories from fat:	22	fat (gm):	2.6
cholesterol (mg):	2	sodium (mg):	281

◆

CURRIED CREAM OF VEGETABLE SOUP

◆

No ordinary cream of vegetable soup this! A careful blend of vegetables, herbs, and spices makes it very full-flavored and zesty.

Makes 7 to 9 Servings:

1 tablespoon non-diet, tub-style margarine
1 cup sweet red pepper, chopped
2 cups onions, coarsely chopped
1 cup carrots, chopped
½ cup celery, chopped
3½ cups tart cooking apples (such as Granny Smith), peeled, cored, and chopped
2½ cups chicken broth (defatted)
1½ tablespoons mild curry powder
½ teaspoon ground allspice
½ teaspoon dried thyme leaves
2⅓ cups boiling potatoes, peeled and diced
3 tablespoons seedless golden raisins
2½ cups beef broth (defatted), divided
¼ cup tomato sauce
1 cup instant non-fat milk powder
2½ cups whole milk
Salt to taste
Chopped fresh cilantro *or* parsley for garnish (optional)

I n a large pot over medium heat, melt margarine. Add the sweet red pepper and onion and cook, stirring, until slightly soft, about 4 minutes. Add carrot, celery, and apples to pot and continue cooking 7 to 10 minutes longer, stirring, until vegetables are limp and most liquid has evaporated from pot.

Stir in the chicken broth, curry powder, allspice, thyme, potatoes, and raisins. Bring to a boil. Reduce heat, cover, and simmer 12 to 15 minutes or until potatoes are tender; stir frequently to prevent potatoes from sticking to pot bottom.

Measure out ¾ cup of vegetables and set aside. Working in 3 batches, transfer remaining mixture to a blender. Blend until thoroughly pureed and smooth; add a little beef broth to batches if mixture is too thick to puree easily. When all soup is pureed, return it to pot along with the ¾ cup of reserved vegetables.

Combine tomato sauce, milk powder, and about ½ cup more beef broth in blender. Blend until completely smooth. Stir tomato mixture into pot, along with remaining beef broth and milk. If soup is too thick, thin with a little water.

Heat soup over medium-high heat, stirring frequently, about 5 minutes longer or until it just comes to a simmer. Add salt if desired.

Just before serving, garnish soup with cilantro or parsley if desired.

Keeps, refrigerated, 3 to 4 days.

Number of Servings: 9 *(data per serving)*

calories:	192	protein (gm):	8.8
% calories from fat:	20	fat (gm):	4.2
cholesterol (mg):	11	sodium (mg):	507

TYROLEAN CABBAGE SOUP

This is a hearty, peasant-style soup perfect for serving with a good, dark bread. Cabbage and caraway seeds are particularly popular ingredients in Tyrolean cooking.

Makes 7 to 8 Servings.

1 tablespoon non-diet, tub-style margarine
2 medium-sized onions, chopped
2 large celery stalks, chopped
1 cup rutabaga, peeled and chopped
1 medium-sized carrot, chopped
1 large tart apple, peeled, cored, and chopped
2 tablespoons all-purpose white flour
5 cups beef broth (defatted), *or* beef bouillon reconstituted from cubes or granules
¼ cup fresh parsley leaves, chopped
7 cups cabbage (about ¾ lb.), very coarsely shredded, divided
2 small pork hocks (about 1¼ lbs.)
¼ cup pearl barley, uncooked
1 tablespoon paprika, preferably imported sweet paprika
2 large bay leaves
½ teaspoon dried thyme leaves
¼ teaspoon black pepper
¼ cup tomato paste
¾ cup water
¼ teaspoon caraway seeds

I n a large pot over medium heat, melt margarine. Add onion, celery, rutabaga, carrot, and apple and cook, stirring until slightly soft, about 5 minutes. Add flour, stirring until smoothly incorporated. Cook, stirring, about 30 seconds. A bit at a time, stir in beef broth until smoothly incorporated into flour mixture.

Add parsley, half of cabbage, pork hocks, barley, paprika, bay leaves, thyme, and black pepper. Bring to a boil. Reduce heat and cover; gently simmer 1 hour, stirring occasionally. Discard pork hocks and bay leaves. Skim fat from soup surface, using a large spoon.

Thoroughly stir together tomato paste and water until smooth and well blended. Stir tomato paste mixture, remaining cabbage, and caraway seeds into pot. Continue simmering, covered, 15 to 20 minutes longer or until cabbage is cooked through but still slightly crisp. Serve immediately, garnished with chopped parsley.

Keeps, refrigerated, 2 or 3 days.

Number of Servings: 8 *(data per serving)*

calories:	143	protein (gm):	8.0
% calories from fat:	28	fat (gm):	4.4
cholesterol (mg):	18	sodium (mg):	412

HERBED CABBAGE SOUP

Makes 4 to 5 Servings.

1 tablespoon non-diet, tub-style margarine
¼ cup fresh chives or green onions (including tops), chopped
1 large onion, chopped
2 tablespoons all-purpose white flour
4 cups chicken stock, *or* broth (defatted)
6 cups cabbage (about ¾ lb.), finely shredded
1 cup all purpose potato cubes, peeled
1 tablespoon fresh tarragon leaves, finely chopped, *or* ¾ teaspoon dried tarragon leaves
¼ teaspoon white pepper (or to taste)
1½ cups 2% milk
Salt to taste
Chopped fresh chives for garnish (optional)

I n a large saucepan over medium heat, melt margarine. Add chives and onions and cook, stirring, until onions are soft, about 5 minutes. Stir in flour and cook, stirring, until smoothly incorporated. Continue cooking, stirring, for 30 seconds longer. Gradually stir in stock until thoroughly and smoothly incorporated into flour mixture. Add cabbage, potato, tarragon, and pepper.

Bring mixture to a boil over medium-high heat. Reduce heat, cover, and simmer about 15 minutes until potato and cabbage are tender; stir frequently to prevent potato from sticking to pan bottom.

Using a measuring cup, scoop up about 2 cups of the mixture and transfer it to blender. Blend until thoroughly pureed, about 1 minute. Return puree to pot. Add milk. Heat, stirring, about 5 minutes longer or until soup is piping hot. Add salt if desired. Garnish servings with chopped fresh chives.

This soup keeps in refrigerator up to 3 days.

Number of Servings: 5 *(data per serving)*

calories:	156	protein (gm):	9.0
% calories from fat:	25	fat (gm):	4.3
cholesterol (mg):	6	sodium (mg):	430

RED ONION AND APPLE SOUP WITH CURRY

Makes 5 to 6 Servings.

- 1 tablespoon non-diet, tub-style margarine
- 1¼ lbs. red onions (about 4 medium-sized), thinly sliced
- 5½ cups chicken stock, *or* broth (defatted)
- 1 cup water
- 2 cups peeled and cored tart cooking apples, coarsely grated or shredded, divided
- ½ cup carrots, finely shredded
- 1 large bay leaf
- 1 teaspoon mild curry powder
- ¼ teaspoon chili powder
- ⅛ teaspoon dried thyme leaves
- ⅛ teaspoon ground allspice
- ¼ teaspoon (generous) black pepper
- Salt to taste
- Chutney for garnish (optional)

I n a large pot, melt margarine over medium heat. Add onions and cook over medium heat, stirring frequently, until soft and slightly translucent. Add a tablespoon or two of stock if necessary to prevent onions from burning. Add remainder of stock, water, 1 cup of apples, and all remaining ingredients except salt and chutney. Bring mixture to a boil over medium-high heat. Cover, lower heat, and simmer about 25 minutes.

Stir in reserved 1 cup of apples and simmer 5 minutes longer. Discard bay leaf. Stir in salt if desired. Garnish each serving with a teaspoon or two of chutney.

Keeps, refrigerated, 3 or 4 days.

Number of Servings: 6 *(data per serving)*

calories:	102	protein (gm):	5.8
% calories from fat:	24	fat (gm):	2.7
cholesterol (mg):	1	sodium (mg):	421

TOMATO BISQUE

Makes 7 to 8 Servings.

1½ teaspoons non-diet, tub-style margarine
1 large onion, chopped
2 large celery stalks, chopped
¼ cup sweet red pepper, chopped
1 small carrot, chopped
2 large garlic cloves, minced
2 tablespoons all-purpose white flour
2½ cups beef broth (defatted)
2 small ham hocks (about 1¼ lbs.)
½ cup potatoes, peeled and diced
1 teaspoon dried thyme leaves
¾ teaspoon ground allspice
¾ teaspoon curry powder
¼ teaspoon black pepper
1 35-oz. can imported Italian (plum) tomatoes, including juice
1 6-oz. can tomato paste
1 teaspoon granulated sugar
1½ cups 1% milk
Salt to taste
Chopped fresh chives for garnish (optional)

In a large pot over medium heat, melt margarine. Add onion, celery, red pepper, carrot, and garlic and cook, stirring, until slightly soft, about 5 minutes. Add flour, stirring until smoothly incorporated. Cook, stirring, about 30 seconds. A bit at a time, stir in beef broth until smoothly incorporated into flour mixture.

Add ham hocks, potato, thyme, allspice, curry powder, and black pepper. Bring to a boil. Reduce heat and cover; gently simmer 15 minutes, stirring occasionally.

Discard ham hocks. In two batches, transfer mixture to blender. Blend on low, then medium speed until thoroughly pureed and smooth. Return puree to pot.

In blender in two batches, blend tomatoes on low speed until finely chopped but not completely pureed. Add to pot. Combine tomato paste, sugar, and milk in blender. Puree until very smooth. Add to pot.

Heat bisque over medium-high heat, stirring frequently, about 5 minutes longer or until it just comes to a simmer. Stir in salt if desired. Serve immediately, garnished with chopped chives.

Keeps, refrigerated, 2 or 3 days.

Number of Servings: 8 *(data per serving)*

calories:	112	protein (gm):	7.1
% calories from fat:	29	fat (gm):	3.6
cholesterol (mg):	16	sodium (mg):	450

ITALIAN GARDEN SOUP

A light, colorful soup, showcasing an appealing blend of "Italian" vegetables and herbs.

Makes 5 to 6 Servings.

1 tablespoon olive oil, preferably extra-virgin
1 large onion, chopped
2 large celery stalks, diced
¼ cup sweet red pepper, diced
2 large garlic cloves, minced
6 cups chicken stock, *or* broth (defatted)
1 cup cooked cannellini, *or* white kidney beans, canned cannellini, *or* Great Northern beans, rinsed and well drained
3 medium-sized carrots, diced
1 bay leaf
¾ teaspoon dried basil leaves
½ teaspoon dried marjoram leaves
¼ teaspoon dried oregano leaves
¼ teaspoon dried thyme leaves
¼ teaspoon white pepper
1 cup mixed yellow squash and zucchini, diced
2 medium-sized fresh plum tomatoes, peeled, seeded, and diced
Chopped fresh chives or parsley for garnish (optional)

In a large pot over medium heat, combine oil, onion, celery, red pepper, and garlic and cook, stirring, until onion is slightly soft, about 5 minutes. Add stock, beans, carrots, bay leaf, basil, marjoram, oregano, thyme, and pepper. Bring mixture to a boil over high heat. Reduce heat and cover; simmer 20 minutes.

Add squash and tomatoes and simmer 5 to 7 minutes longer or until carrots and squash are just tender. Discard bay leaf. Garnish soup servings, with chopped chives or parsley if desired.

Keep, refrigerated, 3 or 4 days.

Number of Servings: 6 *(data per serving)*

calories:	134	protein (gm):	9.0
% calories from fat:	21	fat (gm):	3.2
cholesterol (mg):	1	sodium (mg):	457

HIGH SUMMER SOUP WITH SALSA

◆

This festive, seasonal soup features vegetables bountiful in high summer—yellow squash, corn, and tomatoes. The mild flavor of the squash and corn is a nice foil the for zesty fresh tomato salsa.

◆

Makes 4 to 5 Servings.

Salsa

- 1 very large, fully ripe, vine-ripened tomato, peeled, seeded, and finely diced
- 1 tablespoon fresh chives, finely chopped, *or* green onion (including tops)
- 1 teaspoon red wine vinegar, *or* apple cider vinegar
- ¼ teaspoon salt

Soup

- 1 tablespoon non-diet, tub-style margarine
- 2 large onions, coarsely chopped
- ¼ cup carrot, chopped
- 1 large garlic clove, chopped
- 1 tablespoon all-purpose white flour
- 3 cups chicken stock, *or* broth (defatted)
- 1¼ lbs. yellow squash (3 to 4 medium-sized), chopped
- ½ cup boiling potato, peeled and diced
- ¼ teaspoon powdered mustard
- ⅛ teaspoon white pepper
- 1½ cups fresh or frozen yellow corn kernels, divided
- ½ cup whole milk
- 1½ teaspoons fresh lemon juice
  Finely chopped fresh cilantro leaves for garnish (optional)

A bout 30 minutes before serving time, prepare salsa: Combine all ingredients in a non-corrosive bowl, tossing until mixed. Cover and refrigerate until needed.

In a large pot over medium heat, melt margarine. Add onions, carrot, and garlic and cook, stirring, until onions are limp, about 5 minutes. Stir in flour until incorporated. Cook, stirring, for 30 seconds. Gradually stir in stock until incorporated smoothly. Stir in squash, potato, mustard, pepper, and 1 cup corn.

Bring mixture to a boil over medium-high heat. Lower heat and simmer, uncovered, about 10 minutes or until potato is tender. In batches, transfer mixture to blender. Blend on low speed 10 seconds; then raise speed to high and blend until mixture is completely pureed and smooth.

Return puree, remaining ½ cup corn, milk, and lemon juice to pot. Let mixture return to a simmer, and cook 5 to 8 minutes longer or until corn is tender. Garnish servings with a sprinkling of cilantro if desired. Top the center of each bowl with a heaping tablespoon or two of salsa.

Keeps, refrigerated, 2 or 3 days.

Number of Servings: 5 *(data per serving)*

calories:	158	protein (gm):	7.5
% calories from fat:	22	fat (gm):	3.9
cholesterol (mg):	4	sodium (mg):	734

GREEN ONION-POTATO SOUP WITH DILL

Simple but very good. Use fresh dill weed if at all possible.

Makes 6 to 7 Servings.

1 tablespoon non-diet, tub-style margarine
2½ cups green onions (including tops), chopped
2 tablespoons all-purpose white flour
6 cups chicken stock, *or* broth (defatted), divided
1¾ cups boiling potatoes, peeled and finely cubed
¼ teaspoon white pepper, *or* to taste
2 tablespoons fresh dill weed, *or* 1 tablespoon dried dill weed, finely chopped
¼ cup low-fat plain yogurt
Salt to taste

I n a large saucepan over medium heat, melt margarine. Add green onions and cook, stirring, until soft, about 5 minutes. Stir in flour and cook, stirring, until smoothly incorporated. Cook, stirring, for 30 seconds longer.

Gradually stir in 3 cups stock until thoroughly and smoothly incorporated into flour mixture. Add potatoes, pepper, and dill and bring mixture to a boil over medium-high heat. Reduce heat, cover, and simmer about 12 minutes until potato is tender; stir frequently to prevent potato from sticking to pan bottom.

Using a measuring cup, scoop up about ½ cup of vegetables and liquid and transfer mixture to blender. Add 1 cup more stock and the yogurt. Blend until thoroughly pureed, about 30 seconds. Return puree to pot, stirring, until piping hot *but not boiling*, about 5 minutes. Stir in salt, if desired, and serve.

This soup will keep in refrigerator up to 3 days. Be careful not to allow it to boil during reheating.

Number of Servings: 7 *(data per serving)*

calories:	90	protein (gm):	6.0
% calories from fat:	22	fat (gm):	2.2
cholesterol (mg):	1	sodium (mg):	395

Poultry Soups

Spicy North African-Style Chicken Soup

The tangy flavors and hearty textures of North African cuisine
combine in this chicken soup with a difference. The dish makes a
nice introduction to bulgur wheat, which can be purchased
in the specialty food section of many large grocery stores.
However, if you prefer, brown rice or even white rice can be
substituted. If white rice is used, reduce the cooking time
for the grain to about 20 minutes.

Makes 6 to 7 Servings.

- 2 teaspoons olive oil
- 3 cups red onion (if unavailable, substitute yellow onion), coarsely chopped
- 2 large garlic cloves, minced
- 5 cups chicken stock (pg. 195), *or* broth (defatted), divided
- 1 cup water
- 2 chicken breast halves, skins removed (about 1 lb.)
- 2 large celery stalks, thinly sliced
- ½ cup fresh parsley leaves, finely chopped
- 1 14½ to 16-oz. can tomatoes, including juice
- 1 cinnamon stick, 3-in. long
- 2 large bay leaves
- ¾ teaspoon dried marjoram leaves
- 1 teaspoon dried thyme leaves
- ⅛ teaspoon ground cloves
  - Dash (generous) cayenne pepper
- ¼ teaspoon black pepper
- ½ cup (scant) dry bulgur wheat

In a large pot, combine olive oil, onion, garlic, and 3 tablespoons of chicken stock. Cook over medium heat, stirring frequently, about 5 or 6 minutes or until onion is tender. Add remaining stock, water, chicken, celery, and parsley; then add tomatoes, breaking them up with large spoon. Add cinnamon stick, bay leaves, marjoram, thyme, ground cloves, cayenne, and black pepper. Stir to mix well.

Bring mixture to a boil. Lower heat, cover, and simmer about 35 to 40 minutes or until chicken is tender. With a slotted spoon, remove chicken and reserve it in medium-sized bowl. Remove cinnamon stick and bay leaves and discard. With a large, shallow spoon, skim fat from top of soup and discard.

Bring soup to a boil. Stir in bulgur wheat. Lower heat and simmer an additional 40 to 45 minutes until bulgur is tender. Meanwhile, remove chicken meat from bones, and cut it into bite-sized pieces. When bulgur is tender, return chicken to pot and simmer an additional 2 to 3 minutes.

This soup keeps for 3 to 4 days in refrigerator.

Number of Servings: 7 *(data per serving)*

calories:	138	protein (gm):	12.4
% calories from fat:	18	fat (gm):	2.7
cholesterol (mg):	17	sodium (mg):	429

ALPHABET CHICKEN SOUP

*Kids like the alphabet letters in this traditional chicken soup.
Adults may prefer another small pasta shape.*

Makes 5 to 6 Servings.

2 teaspoons canola, safflower, or corn oil
1 medium-sized onion, finely chopped
1 large garlic clove, minced
5 cups chicken bouillon, reconstituted from
   cubes or granules, divided
2 cups water
2 large chicken breast halves, skins removed
   (about 1 lb.)
2 large carrots, thinly sliced
2 large celery stalks, thinly sliced
2 tablespoons fresh parsley, finely chopped
1 large bay leaf
½ teaspoon dried thyme leaves
⅛ teaspoon ground celery seed
¼ teaspoon black pepper
½ cup alphabet pasta
   Salt to taste

In a Dutch oven or small soup pot, combine vegetable oil, onion, garlic, and 3 tablespoons of chicken bouillon. Cook over medium heat, stirring frequently, until onion is tender, about 5 or 6 minutes. If liquid begins to evaporate, add a bit more broth. Add all remaining ingredients *except* alphabet pasta and salt.

Bring soup to a boil over high heat. Lower heat, cover, and cook about 45 minutes or until chicken is tender. With large, shallow spoon, skim off and discard fat from top of soup. Remove chicken from soup and reserve in medium-sized bowl.

Bring soup to a boil again over high heat. Add alphabet pasta. Lower heat and gently boil 8 to 10 minutes, uncovered, until pasta is tender. Meanwhile, when chicken is cool enough to handle, remove meat from bones and cut into small pieces. When pasta is just cooked through, return chicken to soup. Add salt if desired. Heat an additional 2 to 3 minutes. Remove bay leaf.

After refrigeration, the pasta will thicken this soup. Before reheating, you may want to thin it with a bit more chicken broth.

◆

Number of Servings: 6 *(data per serving)*

calories:	158	protein (gm):	20.0
% calories from fat:	23	fat (gm):	4.0
cholesterol (mg):	55	sodium (mg):	784

CHICKEN-RICE SOUP

Tarragon, along with shredded turnip and parsnip, helps give this soup its rich flavor. Interestingly, the shredded white vegetables masquerade as additional rice.

Makes 7 to 8 Servings.

1 large onion, finely chopped
1 large garlic clove, minced
2 teaspoons canola, safflower, or corn oil
6 cups chicken bouillon, reconstituted from cubes, divided
1 medium-sized parsnip, peeled, trimmed, and grated or shredded
1 medium-sized turnip, peeled, trimmed, and grated or shredded
2 medium-sized carrots, thinly sliced
2 celery stalks, thinly sliced
3 cups water
2 bay leaves
¾ teaspoon dried thyme leaves
½ teaspoon dried tarragon leaves
¼ teaspoon ground celery seed
¼ teaspoon (generous) black pepper
1½ to 2 lbs. bone-in chicken breasts, skins removed
½ cup (scant) uncooked long-grain white rice
Salt to taste

I n a large Dutch oven or soup pot, combine onion, garlic, oil, and 3 tablespoons of chicken bouillon. Cook over medium heat, stirring frequently, until onion is tender, about 5 or 6 minutes. Add all remaining ingredients *except* chicken and rice.

Bring soup to a boil. Cover, lower heat, and simmer about 20 minutes. Add chicken and simmer an additional 45 to 50 minutes or until chicken is very tender and flavors are well blended. Remove soup from heat. With a large, shallow spoon, skim fat from top and discard. Remove chicken breasts and set aside. Remove bay leaves and discard.

Return soup to heat. Add rice. Bring soup to a boil. Cover, lower heat, and simmer 20 to 25 minutes or until rice is tender. Meanwhile, remove chicken meat from bones and cut into small pieces. When rice is tender, return chicken meat to pot. Add salt if desired. Heat an additional 2 minutes.

This soup keeps 3 to 4 days in refrigerator.

Number of Servings: 8 *(data per serving)*

calories:	159	protein (gm):	15.4
% calories from fat:	17	fat (gm):	3.0
cholesterol (mg):	36	sodium (mg):	704

CHICKEN AND CHILI SOUP

Although cheese is relatively high in fat, there's only a small amount per serving in this recipe. To lower the fat content, regular Cheddar and non-fat Cheddar cheese food are used in combination. The green chilies add extra zip and give the soup its spicy South-of-the-Border flavor. This soup is good for lunch and also makes a nice first course with a Mexican-style dinner.

Makes 6 to 7 Servings.

1 teaspoon non-diet, tub-style margarine
1 medium-sized onion, finely chopped
1 large garlic clove, minced
1 large celery stalk, diced
4½ cups chicken broth, *or* stock (defatted), divided
¾ cup skinless cooked chicken breast meat, cut into bite-sized pieces (1 small breast half)
1 4-oz. can chopped green chilies, rinsed and drained
1½ cups small cauliflower pieces
1 cup cooked kidney beans, *or* 1 cup canned kidney beans, drained
2 tablespoons cornstarch
¼ cup cold water
2 ozs. mild Cheddar cheese (about ½ cup), grated
1½ ozs. Alpine Lace non-fat cheese food (about ½ cup), shredded
Chopped fresh chives for garnish (optional)

I n a medium-sized saucepan, melt margarine over medium heat. Add onion, garlic, celery, and 3 tablespoons broth. Cook, stirring frequently, until onion is tender, about 4 to 5 minutes. If liquid begins to evaporate, add a bit more broth. Add remaining broth, cooked chicken, chilies, cauliflower, and kidney beans. Bring mixture to a boil, cover, and simmer about 10 minutes until celery is crisp-tender.

Meanwhile, in a small bowl or cup, combine cornstarch and water. Stir mixture into broth, and cook, stirring until broth thickens, about 1 to 2 minutes. Lower heat so that soup simmers gently.

Stir cheese and cheese food together. In two or three batches, add cheese and cheese food to soup, stirring well with a large spoon after each addition. Stir until regular cheese melts. (The non-fat type will not melt completely.) Continue to gently simmer soup, stirring frequently, about 2 to 3 more minutes; *do not* allow it to come to full boil.

Garnish individual servings with chopped fresh chives if desired.

This soup keeps 1 to 2 days in refrigerator.

Number of Servings: 7 *(data per serving)*

calories:	141	protein (gm):	13.6
% calories from fat:	26	fat (gm):	4.1
cholesterol (mg):	19	sodium (mg):	619

CHICKEN AND CUCUMBER SOUP

◆

Cooked cucumber and tarragon complement each other perfectly in this subtle and pleasing soup.

Makes 4 Servings.

2 teaspoons non-diet, tub-style margarine
1 medium-sized onion, finely chopped
1 small garlic clove, minced
1 scallion, including green top, thinly sliced
3 cups chicken broth (defatted), divided
2 tablespoons all-purpose white flour
½ lb. cooked chicken breast meat (2 medium-sized half-breasts), cut into bite-sized pieces
1 medium-sized cucumber, peeled, seeded, and diced
2 tablespoons fresh parsley leaves, chopped
1 teaspoon lemon juice, preferably fresh
¼ teaspoon (generous) dried tarragon leaves
⅛ teaspoon white pepper
Salt to taste

In a medium-sized saucepan, melt margarine over medium heat. Add onion, garlic, scallion, and 3 tablespoons chicken broth. Cook, stirring occasionally, about 5 or 6 minutes or until onion is tender. If liquid begins to evaporate, add a bit more broth.

Remove pan from heat. With a wooden spoon, stir in flour until smooth and well blended. Return pan to heat, and cook the margarine-flour mixture, stirring, for 1 minute. Gradually add remaining broth, stirring until mixture is smooth. Raise heat and bring mixture to a simmer.

Add all remaining ingredients except salt. Lower heat, cover, and simmer 8 to 15 minutes, depending on degree of crispness you prefer in the cucumbers. Add salt if desired.

This soup keeps 1 to 2 days in refrigerator.

Number of Servings: 4 *(data per serving)*

calories:	169	protein (gm):	22.6
% calories from fat:	23	fat (gm):	4.4
cholesterol (mg):	48	sodium (mg):	390

CHUNKY CHICKEN AND PASTA SOUP

This colorful soup always gets an enthusiastic reception, yet it's very quick and easy to make.

Makes 5 to 6 Servings.

1 tablespoon olive oil

½ lb. chicken breast halves, boned and skinned, cut into ½-in. cubes (meat from 2 medium-sized breast halves)

3½ cups chicken broth (defatted), divided

1 large onion, finely chopped

1 garlic clove, minced

½ large sweet green pepper, diced

½ large sweet red pepper, diced (if unavailable, substitute ½ large sweet green pepper)

1 14½- to 16-oz. can tomatoes (preferably Italian plum), including juice

¼ cup fresh parsley leaves, finely chopped

¾ teaspoon dried basil leaves

½ teaspoon (scant) dried oregano leaves

1 bay leaf

¼ teaspoon black pepper

2 ozs. uncooked vermicelli or thin spaghetti, broken into 2-in. lengths (about 1 cup)

I n a Dutch oven or very large saucepan, combine olive oil and chicken over medium heat. Cook, stirring frequently, until chicken has changed color and begun to brown, about 5 or 6 minutes. With slotted spoon, remove chicken and reserve in small bowl.

Add 2 tablespoons of chicken broth to pan in which chicken was cooked. Stir to combine it with oil remaining in pan. Add onion and garlic and cook about 7 minutes, stirring frequently. Add the sweet green and sweet red pepper and cook, stirring frequently, until onion is tender, about 5 more minutes. If liquid begins to evaporate, add a bit more broth to pan.

Add remaining chicken broth and tomatoes, breaking up tomatoes with large spoon. Add reserved chicken along with parsley, dried basil, oregano, bay leaf, and black pepper. Stir to mix well. Bring to boil. Stir in spaghetti.

Lower heat again and boil gently, covered, 12 to 17 minutes or until spaghetti is tender; stir occasionally. Remove and discard bay leaf.

This soup keeps 2 to 3 days in refrigerator.

Number of Servings: 6 (data per serving)

calories:	190	protein (gm):	18.0
% calories from fat:	21	fat (gm):	4.5
cholesterol (mg):	32	sodium (mg):	390

SPANISH-STYLE VEGETABLE SOUP

◆

While on a trip to Spain, one of us enjoyed several versions of this tasty vegetable-meat soup. For American cooks, the combination of ingredients is unusual, but they yield very flavorful results. The soup should be refrigerated overnight so that the solidified fat can be removed easily and discarded. If you like, the soup can be refrigerated before the potatoes, green beans, and asparagus are added and completed the next day. If fresh asparagus is unavailable, it can be omitted from the recipe; this does change the flavor significantly, but the resulting soup is still unusual and appealing.

◆

Makes 9 to 11 Servings.

2 teaspoons olive oil
1 large onion, finely chopped
2 large garlic cloves, minced
1 medium-sized leek, white part only, well washed and chopped
12 cups water
2 lbs. beef soup bones
4 beef bouillon cubes
1 8-oz. package country ham, trimmed of all fat and cut into bite-sized pieces
½ cup dry lima beans or navy beans, rinsed and picked over
3 large romaine lettuce leaves, coarsely shredded
½ cup fresh parsley leaves, finely chopped
2 medium-sized carrots, thinly sliced
2 large celery stalks, including leaves, thinly sliced
2 large bay leaves
1 teaspoon dried thyme leaves
¼ teaspoon black pepper, or to taste
1 large boneless chicken breast half (½-¾ lbs.), skin and fat removed

2 large boiling potatoes, peeled or unpeeled, cut
   into ¾-in. cubes
6 to 7 medium-sized asparagus spears, cut
   crosswise into 1-in. slices, tips and tender
   green parts only
1½ cups fresh 1-in. string bean pieces
   Salt to taste

I n a large soup pot, combine olive oil, onion, garlic, and leek. Cook over medium heat, stirring frequently, until onion is tender, about 5 or 6 minutes. Add water, beef bones, bouillon cubes, ham, lima beans, lettuce, parsley, carrots, celery, bay leaves, thyme, and pepper. Bring mixture to a boil. Lower heat, cover, and simmer about 40 minutes.

Add chicken and simmer an additional hour. Remove chicken and reserve. Add potatoes, asparagus, and green beans. Simmer an additional 30 to 40 minutes or until vegetables and beans are tender. Remove and discard beef bones and bay leaves. Cut chicken meat into pieces and return it to soup.

Refrigerate soup overnight. Remove and discard solidified fat from top of soup. Reheat over medium heat, stirring frequently, to prevent soup from sticking to bottom of pot. Add salt if desired.

This soup keeps 4 to 5 days in refrigerator.

Number of Servings: 11 *(data per serving)*

calories:	147	protein (gm):	14.8
% calories from fat:	21	fat (gm):	3.4
cholesterol (mg):	26	sodium (mg):	594

CURLY ENDIVE AND CHICKEN SOUP

Curly endive tends to be a little bitter when eaten fresh, but the flavor mellows considerably during cooking. In this unusual chicken-vegetable-noodle soup, it adds a distinctive and appealing taste as well as attractive bits of green color.

Makes 8 to 10 Servings.

2¾ lbs. bony chicken pieces (wings, backs, etc.)

1 lb. chicken breast halves, skin removed

8½ cups dry chicken broth (defatted), *or* chicken bouillon reconstituted from cubes or granules

3½ cups water

½ cup dry white wine

2 large onions, finely chopped

2 large carrots, finely chopped

2 large celery stalks, finely chopped

2 large bay leaves

1¼ teaspoons dried marjoram leaves

1 teaspoon dried basil leaves

½ teaspoon dried thyme leaves

1 teaspoon black pepper

3 large boiling potatoes, peeled and diced

¾ lb. (generous) curly endive or chicory (1 very large head), washed and drained

1½ cups canned, peeled Italian (plum) tomatoes, including juice, chopped

Salt to taste

2 cups dry fettuccini noodles, cooked *al dente* according to manufacturer's directions, then drained

Combine chicken pieces, chicken breast, broth, water, wine, onions, carrots, celery, bay leaf, marjoram, basil, thyme, and pepper in a very large pot. Bring mixture to a boil over medium-high heat. Lower heat and simmer, covered, for 1 hour. Remove chicken breast halves and set aside to cool. Add potatoes. Continue simmering mixture, covered, 30 minutes longer, stirring occasionally.

Meanwhile, trim off and discard tough stems and tough outer leaves of endive. Finely chop endive; there should be enough to yield about 8 to 8½ lightly packed cups. Put chopped endive in colander and wash thoroughly under cool running water. Set aside to drain.

Skim off and discard fat from soup, using large, shallow spoon. Remove and discard bony chicken pieces from pot, using slotted spoon.

Stir endive, tomatoes, and salt (if desired) into pot.

Bring mixture to a boil, stirring. Lower heat and simmer, covered, about 12 to 15 minutes or until endive is almost tender.

Remove chicken breast meat from bones and cut into bite-sized pieces. Stir chicken meat and cooked fettuccini into soup. Continue cooking, covered, 2 to 3 minutes longer or until chicken and noodles are heated through.

Keeps, refrigerated, 1 to 2 days.

Number of Servings: 10 (data per serving)

calories:	166	protein (gm):	17.9
% calories from fat:	11	fat (gm):	2.1
cholesterol (mg):	35	sodium (mg):	471

HOME-STYLE TURKEY-VEGETABLE SOUP

◆

*A homey, stick-to-the-ribs soup that's very popular with families.
The recipe is designed to yield a lot of soup since it disappears fast
and is great reheated.*

◆

Makes 9 to 11 Servings.

4 lbs. turkey wings (3 to 4 medium-sized wings)
3 cups water
7 cups chicken broth (defatted), *or* bouillon
reconstituted from chicken bouillon cubes
3 large onions, coarsely chopped
1 cup rutabaga or turnip, peeled and diced
1 cup celery, chopped
1 cup cabbage, finely chopped
¼ cup fresh parsley leaves, chopped
¼ cup pearl barley
4 to 5 carrots, cut crosswise into ⅛-in.-thick
slices
2 stalks celery, cut crosswise into ⅛-in.-thick
slices
¼ cup dry, medium-sized macaroni elbows
¼ teaspoon dried marjoram leaves
⅛ teaspoon dried thyme leaves
½ teaspoon salt, or to taste
½ teaspoon black pepper, or to taste
1½ cups frozen yellow corn kernels
1 15-oz. can tomatoes (including juice), broken
up with spoon
1 16-oz. can white beans, or cannellini beans,
drained

Combine turkey wings, water, chicken broth, onions, rutabaga,
chopped celery, cabbage, parsley, and barley in 6-quart or larger
soup pot and bring to a boil over high heat. Lower heat, cover pot, and
simmer mixture for 1 hour and 20 to 30 minutes or until turkey wings
are tender.

Remove turkey wings from pot and set aside. When they are cool enough to handle, remove meat and cut into bite-sized pieces. Using large, shallow spoon, skim off and discard all fat from soup surface. Add carrots, sliced celery, macaroni, marjoram, thyme, salt, and pepper to pot. Bring mixture to a simmer and continue cooking, covered, 45 minutes.

Stir in corn, tomatoes, reserved turkey meat, and beans and simmer about 20 minutes longer or until carrots are tender.

This soup may be refrigerated up to 3 days for later use. Thin it with a little water if necessary.

Number of Servings: 11 *(data per serving)*

calories:	216	protein (gm):	18.2
% calories from fat:	13	fat (gm):	3.1
cholesterol (mg):	26	sodium (mg):	490

MALAYSIAN-STYLE CHICKEN AND SCALLION SOUP

The exotic flavor of this Malaysian-style soup comes from ginger, lemon, anise, cilantro, and cumin, which are often used together in Far Eastern cuisines.

Makes 5 to 6 Servings.

5½ cups chicken stock (pg. 195), *or* broth (defatted), divided

2 tablespoons fresh ginger root, coarsely chopped

1 large garlic clove, minced

1 lemon slice, ¼-in. thick

½ teaspoon (generous) anise seeds

½ teaspoon coriander seeds

¼ teaspoon cumin seeds

¼ teaspoon whole black peppercorns

2 medium-sized skinless, boneless chicken breast halves, cut into 1-in.-long by ⅛-in.-thick strips

1 cup green onions (scallions), including tops, coarsely shredded

Chopped fresh cilantro for garnish (optional)

I n a large pot over high heat, combine 5 cups stock, ginger root, garlic, lemon slice, anise, coriander, cumin, and peppercorns. Bring mixture to a boil; lower heat and simmer, covered, 30 minutes.

Meanwhile, in a small saucepan, combine remaining ½ cup stock and chicken pieces. Bring to a simmer over medium-high heat. Lower heat and gently poach chicken, covered, 2 to 3 minutes or until pieces are just cooked through. Turn out chicken into a colander, discarding stock. Thoroughly rinse chicken to remove any scum. Set aside to drain.

Strain the simmered broth-herb mixture through a very fine sieve, discarding seasoning ingredients. Rinse out large pot previously used and return strained broth and green onions to it. Simmer 2 minutes. Add chicken and simmer 1 minute longer.

Serve in small bowls or cups. Garnish servings with chopped cilantro leaves if desired.

Number of Servings: 6 *(data per serving)*

calories:	126	protein (gm):	22.5
% calories from fat:	17	fat (gm):	2.4
cholesterol (mg):	49	sodium (mg):	433

MULLIGATAWNY

Colorful and lightly spiced with curry powder, this popular soup originated in India. Today, however, versions can be found from the British Isles to the Bahamas.

Makes 4 to 6 Servings.

2 teaspoons canola, safflower, or corn oil
2 large onions, coarsely chopped
2 large celery stalks, coarsely chopped
1 large garlic clove, minced
4 cups chicken stock (pg. 195), *or* broth (defatted)
2 large Winesap or other tart, flavorful apples, peeled and coarsely chopped
2 medium carrots, coarsely chopped
¼ cup fresh parsley leaves, coarsely chopped
2 tablespoons sweet red pepper (if unavailable, substitute sweet green pepper), coarsely chopped
1 cup water
½ cup boiling potatoes, peeled and diced
2½ teaspoons curry powder
1 teaspoon chili powder
½ teaspoon ground allspice
¼ teaspoon dried thyme leaves
¼ teaspoon black pepper, preferably freshly ground
1½ lbs. bony chicken pieces (wings, backs, etc.)
1 lb. (2 medium) chicken breast halves, skin removed
1¼ cups canned tomatoes, chopped
Salt to taste
Finely chopped fresh parsley leaves for garnish (optional)

Combine oil, onions, celery, and garlic in large pot. Cook over medium heat, stirring, 4 to 5 minutes until onions are limp. Add tablespoon of chicken stock if needed to prevent vegetables from burning. Add apples, carrots, parsley, and sweet peppers and cook, stirring, 3 to 4 minutes longer. Stir in remaining stock, water, potatoes, curry powder, chili powder, allspice, thyme, and pepper. Add chicken. Bring mixture to a boil; then lower heat and simmer, covered, 1 hour and 5 to 10 minutes.

Remove pot from heat. Remove chicken from pot; discard bony pieces and set breasts aside to cool. Skim off and discard fat on soup surface, using large, shallow spoon. Stir in tomatoes.

Using a measuring cup, scoop about 2 cups vegetables and liquid from pot and transfer to blender or food processor. Blend or process until mixture is completely pureed. Return puree to pot.

When chicken breasts are cool enough to handle, remove meat from bones and cut into bite-sized pieces. Return it to pot, and add salt if desired. Reheat mixture until piping hot. Garnish with parsley.

Keeps, refrigerated, 3 days.

Number of Servings: 6 *(data per serving)*

calories:	208	protein (gm):	23.5
% calories from fat:	19	fat (gm):	4.4
cholesterol (mg):	51	sodium (mg):	432

OLD-FASHIONED CHICKEN-VEGETABLE SOUP

A homey, heartwarming soup like grandma used to make.

Makes 6 to 7 Servings.

6 to 8	medium-sized scallions
1	tablespoon non-diet, tub-style margarine
⅓	cup fresh parsley leaves, chopped
2	medium celery stalks, finely chopped
1	cup green cabbage, shredded
6½	cups chicken broth (defatted), *or* chicken bouillon reconstituted from cubes or granules
1½	lbs. bony chicken parts (wings, backs, etc.)
1	lb. chicken breast halves, skin removed
3	medium-sized carrots, cut into ⅛-in.-thick slices
1	large stalk celery, cut into ⅛-in-thick slices
1	small rutabaga, peeled and cut into ¼-in. cubes
2	cups small cauliflower florets, coarsely chopped
1	cup boiling potatoes, peeled and diced
¼	teaspoon (generous) black pepper
1¼	cups cooked medium-sized egg noodles
	Salt to taste

Trim root ends from scallions and discard. Trim off green tops and coarsely chop them. Cut white portions crosswise into ½-in. lengths. Set scallions aside.

Melt margarine in a 4- to 5-quart soup pot over medium heat. Stir in scallion tops, parsley, and chopped celery and cook 4 to 5 minutes or until vegetables are limp. Add cabbage, chicken broth, chicken parts and breasts and bring to a boil.

Reduce heat and gently simmer mixture, covered, for 1 hour and 15 minutes. Remove chicken pieces from pot and discard bony parts. Set chicken breasts aside to cool. Skim off and discard fat from soup surface, using a large, shallow spoon. Add reserved scallion white parts, carrots, sliced celery, rutabaga, cauliflower, potatoes, and pepper. Cover pot and simmer 45 minutes, stirring occasionally.

Meanwhile, when chicken breasts are cool enough to handle, remove meat from bones and cut into bite-sized chunks. Stir chicken meat and noodles into pot. Continue simmering 3 to 4 minutes, until chicken and noodles are heated through. Add salt if desired.

Keeps, refrigerated, 1 to 2 days.

Number of Servings: 7 *(data per serving)*

calories:	206	protein (gm):	23.4
% calories from fat:	19	fat (gm):	4.4
cholesterol (mg):	53	sodium (mg):	492

CLASSIC CHICKEN NOODLE SOUP

A favorite of kids and adults alike.

Makes 5 to 6 Servings.

   3 lbs. bony chicken pieces (wings, backs, etc.)

6½ cups chicken stock (pg. 195), *or* broth (defatted)

   1 large whole onion

   1 large carrot, halved crosswise

   1 large stalk celery, halved crosswise

   1 small turnip, peeled and halved (optional)

   1 large bay leaf

½ to ¾ teaspoon black pepper

  ¼ teaspoon dried thyme leaves

  ¼ teaspoon dried marjoram leaves

   3 tablespoons fresh parsley leaves, chopped

   2 cups uncooked commercial egg noodles

     Salt to taste

     Finely chopped fresh parsley for garnish (optional)

Combine all ingredients, except noodles, salt, and parsley used for garnishing, in a 4- to 5-quart pot over medium heat. Slowly bring mixture to a boil, covered. Lower heat and simmer mixture, covered, 50 to 60 minutes.

Turn out mixture into a colander set over a large bowl; let stand until all broth drains into bowl. Rinse out soup pot previously used. Strain reserved broth through a fine sieve back into pot previously used.

Finely dice the cooked carrot and celery pieces and return them to pot. When chicken is cool enough to handle, remove meat from bones and cut into bite-sized pieces. Return meat to pot. Using a large, shallow spoon, skim off and discard fat from soup surface. (Alternatively, at this point, cover and refrigerate broth for later use. It can be stored up to 48 hours. Before using, carefully skim off and discard fat from soup surface.)

When ready to serve soup, put noodles in a large pot of rapidly boiling, salted water and boil until just cooked through, according to package directions. Turn noodles out into a colander until well drained. Then add them to soup, which has just been brought to a boil over medium-high heat, and simmer for 3 or 4 minutes longer. Add salt if desired. Sprinkle soup with parsley.

Number of Servings: 6 *(data per serving)*

calories:	380	protein (gm):	36.5
% calories from fat:	29	fat (gm):	12.3
cholesterol (mg):	113	sodium (mg):	519

FISH & SHELLFISH SOUPS

WHITE FISH CHOWDER

Although this soup calls for flounder, any other mild-tasting fish such as orange roughy or halibut may be substituted.

Makes 5 or 6 Servings.

2 teaspoons non-diet, tub-style margarine
1 large onion, finely chopped
1 large garlic clove, chopped
1 large stalk celery, diced

2 cups fish stock (see pg. 201), *or* 2 cups
  vegetable bouillon reconstituted from packets
  or cubes, *or* 2 cups chicken bouillon
  reconstituted from cubes or packets, divided
2 cups 2% milk, divided
2½ cups peeled ¾-in. potato cubes (about 1 large
  potato)
1 cup frozen lima beans
1 large carrot, diced
1½ teaspoons dried basil leaves
½ teaspoon dried marjoram leaves
¼ teaspoon dried thyme leaves
¼ teaspoon mustard powder
¼ teaspoon ground celery seed
¼ teaspoon white pepper
1 tablespoon plus 1 teaspoon cornstarch
1 lb. (fresh or frozen and thawed) skinless
  flounder fillets
1 cup frozen corn kernels
  Salt to taste

I n a large saucepan or small Dutch oven, combine margarine,
onion, garlic, celery, and 2 tablespoons of stock. Cook 5 or 6
minutes at medium heat, stirring frequently, until onion is tender. If liquid
begins to evaporate, add a bit more stock.

Add remaining stock, 1 cup milk, potatoes, lima beans, carrot, basil,
marjoram, thyme, mustard powder, celery seed, and pepper. Bring to a boil
over medium-high heat, stirring occasionaly. Cover pan. Lower heat and
simmer about 15 minutes or until potatoes are tender. While soup is cooking, cut flounder fillets into 1-in. pieces and set aside.

In a small cup, mix together cornstarch and remaining 1 cup of milk.
Add to soup. Raise heat to medium-high. Cook soup, stirring frequently,
until it boils and thickens, about 3 or 4 minutes. Lower heat to medium-low.

Add flounder and corn to soup. Stir to mix well. Cook soup an additional 5 or 6 minutes or until flounder flakes easily with edge of large spoon.
Add salt if desired.

This soup keeps 2 to 3 days in refrigerator.

Number of Servings: 6 *(data per serving)*

calories:	244	protein (gm):	27.7
% calories from fat:	19	fat (gm):	5.2
cholesterol (mg):	37	sodium (mg):	248

MANHATTAN-STYLE CLAM CHOWDER

Quick, easy, and tasty!

Makes 5 to 6 Servings.

2 teaspoons non-diet, tub-style margarine
1 large onion, finely chopped
1 small clove garlic, minced
2 large celery stalks, including leaves, diced
2 6½-oz. cans chopped clams, including juice
  Water
½ large green pepper, diced
1 large potato, peeled and diced
1 16-oz. can stewed tomatoes
2 cups tomato juice
  Dash cayenne pepper
1 bay leaf
½ teaspoon dried thyme leaves
½ teaspoon sugar
¼ teaspoon dried marjoram leaves
⅛ teaspoon black pepper

In a large, heavy saucepan or Dutch oven, melt margarine. Add onion, garlic, and celery. Cook vegetables over medium heat, stirring frequently, until onion is tender, about 6 minutes. If vegetables begin to stick, lower heat.

Drain liquid from clams (reserving clams) into a measuring cup and add enough water to make 1¾ cups of liquid. Add this liquid to pan, along with green pepper and potato. Bring to a boil. Cover, lower heat, and simmer 10 to 12 minutes, stirring occasionally, or until potato is tender. Add clams and all remaining ingredients, breaking up tomatoes with a spoon. Re-cover and bring to a boil. Lower heat and simmer about 5 minutes longer, until flavors are well blended. Remove and discard bay leaf.

This soup keeps 2 to 3 days in refrigerator.

Number of Servings: 6 *(data per serving)*

calories:	101	protein (gm):	7.2
% calories from fat:	20	fat (gm):	2.3
cholesterol (mg):	38	sodium (mg):	479

QUICK AND EASY MANHATTAN-STYLE FISH CHOWDER WITH VEGETABLES

Nothing could be simpler than this fish chowder. Yet with its flavor of the sea and vegetable-rich texture, it makes a great dinner entree.

Makes 5 to 6 Servings.

1 large onion, finely chopped

2 celery stalks, including leaves, coarsely chopped

2 teaspoons non-diet, tub-style margarine

2 cups chicken bouillon reconstituted from cubes or granules, divided

4 cups reduced-sodium tomato juice, *or* regular tomato juice

1 large carrot, very thinly sliced

1½ cups 1-in. frozen French-style green beans

1½ cups loose-pack frozen corn kernels

1 large potato, peeled and diced

1 bay leaf

½ teaspoon (generous) dried thyme leaves

½ teaspoon dried marjoram leaves

¼ teaspoon powdered mustard

Dash cayenne pepper

¼ teaspoon (generous) black pepper

10 to 12 ozs. fresh (or frozen and thawed) skinless fillets of flounder or halibut, cut into ¾-in. pieces

Salt to taste

I n a Dutch oven or small soup pot, combine onion, celery, margarine, and 3 tablespoons of chicken bouillon. Cook over medium heat, stirring frequently, until onion is tender, about 6 or 7 minutes. If liquid begins to evaporate, add a bit more bouillon.

Add remaining bouillon, tomato juice, carrot, green beans, corn, potato, bay leaf, thyme, marjoram, powdered mustard, cayenne pepper, and black pepper. Bring soup to a boil. Cover, lower heat, and simmer 20 to 25 minutes or until vegetables are tender.

Stir in fish. Cook an additional 3 or 4 minutes or until fish flakes easily with edge of large metal spoon. Add salt if desired. Remove and discard bay leaf.

This soup keeps 1 or 2 days in refrigerator.

Number of Servings: 6 *(data per serving)*

calories:	185	protein (gm):	16.7
% calories from fat:	15	fat (gm):	3.0
cholesterol (mg):	19	sodium (mg):	378

Nova Scotia Seafood Chowder

Hearty chowders are a hallmark of the cuisine in Canada's Atlantic Provinces. There's a great variety in these soups, which are milk-based like their New England counterparts. Some are thick and rich. Others are no thicker than whole milk. And the type and combination of seafood used depend on the day's catch. If you can purchase small quantities of fish and shellfish, you can combine about a pound of mixed seafood in this chowder. Otherwise, use a pound's worth of two of the called-for seafood-fish ingredients.

Makes 5 to 6 Servings.

- 2 teaspoons non-diet, tub-style margarine
- 1 large onion, finely chopped
- 1 large garlic clove, chopped
- 1 large stalk celery, diced
- 2 cups fish stock (see pg. 201), *or* 2 cups clam juice, divided
- 2 cups whole milk*
- 2½ cups peeled ¾-in. potato cubes (about 1 large potato)
- 2 cups ¾-in. cauliflower pieces
- 1 large carrot, diced
- 1½ teaspoons dried basil leaves
- ½ teaspoon dried marjoram leaves
- ¼ teaspoon dried thyme leaves
- ¼ teaspoon mustard powder
- ¼ teaspoon (generous) ground celery seed
- ¼ teaspoon (scant) white pepper
- 8 ozs. (fresh or frozen and thawed) skinless mild white fish fillets, such as flounder
- 1 tablespoon plus 1 teaspoon cornstarch
- 4 ozs. (fresh or frozen and thawed) small cooked shrimp
- 4 ozs. crab or king crab meat
  Salt to taste

I n a large saucepan or small Dutch oven, combine margarine, onion, garlic, celery, and 2 tablespoons of stock. Cook 5 or 6 minutes over medium heat or until onion is tender. If liquid begins to evaporate, add a bit more stock.

Add remaining stock, 1 cup of milk, potatoes, cauliflower, carrot, basil, marjoram, thyme, mustard, celery seed, and pepper. Bring to a boil over medium-high heat, stirring occasionally. Cover pot. Lower heat and simmer about 15 minutes or until potatoes are tender. While soup is cooking, cut fish into 1-in. pieces and set aside.

In a large cup, mix cornstarch and remaining 1 cup of milk. Add to soup. Raise heat to medium-high. Cook soup, stirring frequently, until it boils and thickens, about 1 or 2 minutes. Lower heat to medium-low.

Add seafood and fish to soup. Stir to mix well. Add salt if desired. Simmer soup an additional 4 or 5 minutes or until fish flakes easily with edge of large spoon.

This soup keeps in refrigerator 1 or 2 days.

Number of Servings: 6 (data per serving)

calories:	215	protein (gm):	23.4
% calories from fat:	25	fat (gm):	6.0
cholesterol (mg):	82	sodium (mg):	348

---

*Note: To reduce fat, this soup can be made with 2% milk.

SHRIMP AND VEGETABLE CHOWDER

◆

Easy, flavorful, and full of contrasting textures.

◆

Makes 5 to 6 Servings.

  2 teaspoons non-diet, tub-style margarine
  1 medium-sized onion, finely chopped
  1 large garlic clove, minced
  3 cups chicken stock (pg. 195), *or* broth (defatted), divided
1½ cups frozen corn kernels
  1 cup 1-in. cauliflower pieces
  1 cup potato, peeled and diced
  1 cup zucchini, diced
  1 large carrot, diced
  1 medium-sized sweet green pepper, diced
 ½ medium-sized sweet red pepper, diced (if unavailable, substitute sweet green pepper)
 ⅓ cup dry sherry
 ¾ teaspoon dried basil leaves
 ½ teaspoon (scant) dried thyme leaves
 ¼ teaspoon dried marjoram leaves
 ¼ teaspoon chili powder
 ¼ teaspoon powdered mustard
   Dash cayenne pepper
 ⅛ teaspoon black pepper
1½ cups small cooked shrimp (about 7½ ozs.)
1½ tablespoons cornstarch
 ¼ cup cold water
  1 8-oz. can tomato sauce
 ½ cup whole milk
   Salt to taste

I n a large saucepan or small pot, melt margarine over medium heat. Add onion and garlic and 2 tablespoons of stock. Cook, stirring frequently, until onion is soft, about 5 minutes. If liquid begins to evaporate, add a bit more stock.

Add remaining stock, corn, cauliflower, potato, zucchini, carrot, green pepper, red pepper, sherry, basil, thyme, marjoram, chili powder, powdered mustard, cayenne pepper, and black pepper. Bring mixture to a boil. Cover, lower heat, and simmer about 5 minutes.

Add shrimp and continue cooking an additional 5 to 10 minutes or until vegetables are tender. Meanwhile, in a small bowl, stir cornstarch and water together until thoroughly blended. Add cornstarch-water mixture to liquid in pot. Raise heat slightly and cook, stirring frequently, until stock thickens and boils, about 1 to 2 minutes.

Lower heat again. Stir in tomato sauce and milk. Add salt if desired. Heat soup an additional 4 or 5 minutes.

This soup keeps in refrigerator 2 to 3 days.

Number of Servings: 6 *(data per serving)*

calories:	190	protein (gm):	14.0
% calories from fat:	14	fat (gm):	2.9
cholesterol (mg):	72	sodium (mg):	560

SHERRIED CRAB AND MUSHROOM BISQUE

Succulent, sweet crab meat and fresh mushrooms complement one another nicely in this elegant soup. Although the sherry helps bring out the rich, mellow taste, it may be omitted if you wish.

Makes 5 to 6 Servings.

- 1 tablespoon non-diet, tub-style margarine, divided
- 1⅓ lbs. fresh mushrooms, trimmed and sliced, divided
- ⅔ cup onions, chopped
- 2 tablespoons celery with leaves, chopped
- 2 tablespoons carrot, chopped
- 1½ tablespoons all-purpose white flour
- 2½ cups chicken stock (pg. 195), *or* broth (defatted), divided
- ¾ cup boiling potatoes, peeled and diced
- ⅛ teaspoon dried thyme leaves
- ⅛ teaspoon white pepper
- 1 tablespoon tomato paste
- 1½ teaspoons reduced-salt soy sauce
- 1⅓ cups whole milk*
- 6 ozs. fresh lump crab meat, all bits of cartilage and shell removed
- 1 tablespoon fresh chives, finely chopped (optional)
- 2 tablespoons dry or medium-dry sherry

In a large pot, combine half the margarine and a generous half of the mushrooms over medium-low heat. Cook, stirring until mushrooms begin to release their juices. Increase heat to medium-high and continue cooking 4 to 5 minutes longer or until most juice evaporates from the pot.

Turn out cooked mushrooms into a bowl and reserve. Add remaining margarine and mushrooms, onions, celery, and carrots to pot. Return to heat, medium-low, and cook about 6 minutes longer until onions and mushrooms are limp. Stir in flour until smoothly incorporated. Continue cooking, stirring, 1 minute longer.

Add 1½ cups chicken stock, potato, thyme, and pepper. Bring mixture to a boil over medium-high heat. Lower heat, cover, and simmer, stirring frequently to prevent potatoes from sticking, until potatoes are tender, about 10 minutes.

Transfer contents of pot to a blender. Add tomato paste and blend until mixture is completely pureed and smooth. Return puree to pot along with remaining chicken stock, soy sauce, milk, reserved cooked mushrooms, crab meat, chives, and sherry. Bring mixture just to a simmer and serve immediately in small bowls.

Keeps 24 hours in refrigerator.

◆

Number of Servings: 6 *(data per serving)*

calories:	161	protein (gm):	12.7
% calories from fat:	27	fat (gm):	4.9
cholesterol (mg):	36	sodium (mg):	395

◆

*Note: To lower fat in recipe even further, substitute 2% milk for whole milk.

LIGHT SALMON BISQUE WITH DILL

Dill weed complements the flavor of fresh salmon nicely in this light, tempting bisque.

Makes 4 to 5 Servings.

2½ cups fish stock (pg. 201), *or* bottled clam juice (if unavailable, substitute chicken broth), divided

8 ozs. fresh, boneless North Atlantic or king salmon fillet

2 teaspoons non-diet, tub-style margarine

1 cup onions, chopped

¼ cup celery with leaves, chopped

2 tablespoons carrot, chopped

1 tablespoon all-purpose white flour

¼ teaspoon (generous) dry mustard

⅛ teaspoon (generous) white pepper

1½ cups boiling potatoes, peeled and coarsely chopped

1 tablespoon tomato paste

1¼ cups whole milk

2½ teaspoons fresh lemon juice

½ teaspoon salt, or to taste

1 tablespoon fresh dill weed (coarse stems removed), finely chopped *or* 1½ teaspoons dried dill weed

Sprigs of fresh dill weed for garnish (optional)

I n a large pot, bring ½ cup fish stock or clam juice to a simmer over medium-low heat. Add salmon fillet, skin side down. Lower heat and gently poach fish, covered, 5 to 7 minutes or until just cooked through (turns opaque) at thickest part and beginning to flake. Immediately remove fish to a bowl, laying it skin side up. When fish is cool enough to handle, lift off skin with fork and discard it. Strain poaching liquid through a fine sieve over the fish.

Wipe out pot and add margarine, onions, celery, and carrots to it. Cook over medium heat, stirring frequently, until onions are limp, about

4 minutes. Stir in flour until incorporated. Cook, stirring, 30 seconds. Gradually stir in remaining stock until incorporated smoothly into flour. Stir in mustard, pepper, and potatoes.

Bring mixture to a boil over medium-high heat. Lower heat and simmer, uncovered and stirring occasionally, about 12 minutes or until potatoes are tender. Meanwhile, using fork, flake salmon into very fine pieces.

In two batches, blend cooked vegetable-broth mixture and tomato paste in a blender until completely pureed and smooth. Return puree, milk, lemon juice, salt, and dill weed to pot. Add flaked salmon. Let mixture return to a simmer and serve immediately. Garnish servings with sprigs of dill weed if desired.

Keeps 1 to 2 days in refrigerator.

Number of Servings: 5 *(data per serving)*

calories:	211	protein (gm):	17.0
% calories from fat:	29	fat (gm):	6.7
cholesterol (mg):	28	sodium (mg):	489

Maryland Crab Soup

Except in Creole and Cajun cookery and in the San Francisco dish cioppino, crab is not often featured in spicy soups in the United States. This deliciously peppery Maryland specialty is an obvious exception. Numerous versions of the dish can be found throughout the Chesapeake Bay area, particularly in seafood restaurants. Like the gumbos typical in Deep South cookery, this soup derives its rich, distinctive character from the melding of a variety of ingredients—smoked pork, beef stock, vegetables, a unique blend of herbs and spices, and, of course, the crab. And, as in the case of gumbos, the resulting dish is robust, earthy, and very satisfying. The soup is normally quite piquant if not downright hot. If you prefer a milder, less zippy version, add the smaller amount of Old Bay seasoning called for in the recipe. (Old Bay is a popular herb and spice blend used with crabs and other seafood in the Chesapeake region. If Old Bay seasoning is unavailable, see note at the end of the recipe.)

Makes 7 or 8 Servings.

2 ¼-in.-thick slices of slab bacon, finely diced
1 teaspoon non-diet, tub-style margarine
2 large onions, finely chopped
2 large carrots, finely chopped
2 large celery stalks, finely chopped
½ cup fresh parsley leaves, finely chopped
4 cups beef stock, *or* beef broth (defatted)
2½ cups fish stock (see pg. 201), *or* bottled clam juice, *or* chicken broth
2 cups water
1 small ham hock (about ½ lb.)
2 large bay leaves
½ teaspoon powdered mustard
*1 to 2 tablespoons Old Bay seasoning, or to taste
3 cups boiling potatoes, peeled and finely diced
2½ cups canned imported Italian (plum) tomatoes, including juice
1 cup fresh or frozen whole kernel corn
12 ozs. fresh backfin crab meat, carefully picked over to remove cartilage and shell

In a large pot, fry bacon over medium-high heat until cooked through and almost crisp. Add margarine, onions, carrots, celery, and parsley to pot and cook, stirring, 4 to 5 minutes until onions are limp; add a tablespoon or two of beef stock if needed to prevent vegetables from burning.

Add remainder of beef stock, fish stock, water, ham hock, bay leaves, powdered mustard, and Old Bay seasoning. Bring mixture to a boil; then lower heat and simmer, covered, 10 minutes. Stir potatoes into pot and continue simmering, covered, about 20 minutes longer or until they are very tender.

Add tomatoes, breaking them up with a spoon, and then add corn. Heat soup over medium heat, covered, about 10 minutes longer or until piping hot. Discard ham hock and bay leaves. Gently stir in crab meat, being careful not to break up the lumps. Continue cooking until crab is heated to piping hot and serve.

The soup may also be refrigerated up to 36 hours and reheated if desired.

Number of Servings: 8   *(data per serving)*

calories:	213	protein (gm):	18.5
% calories from fat:	18	fat (gm):	4.3
cholesterol (mg):	45	sodium (mg):	639

---

*Note: If Old Bay seasoning mix is unavailable, its flavor can be approximated by substituting the following: ½ teaspoon celery salt, ½ teaspoon paprika, generous ½ teaspoon celery seed, ½ teaspoon ground mustard, generous ¼ teaspoon black pepper, ⅛ to ¼ teaspoon crushed dried red (hot) pepper, ⅛ teaspoon ground cloves, and a generous pinch each of ground mace and ground ginger.

Mussel Soup With Saffron

Brightly colored bits of vegetables and a savory broth bring out the flavor of the mussels in this tempting, eye-catching soup. It should be served immediately, as the colors and flavors begin to fade if the soup is allowed to stand.

Note that we recommend "cultured" mussels in this recipe. These are commercially raised in off-bottom beds, which means they tend to be less sandy and easier to clean than "uncultured" mussels. However, uncultured mussels can certainly be used if washed carefully.

Note that if mussels are purchased in plastic bags, they may tend to "gape" from being out of water. Most "gapers" will close up during the cleaning and soaking process; discard any that don't.

Makes 4 or 5 Servings.

2¼   lbs. fresh mussels, preferably cultured
1¼   cups bottled clam juice
¾   cup water
⅔   cup dry white wine
2   teaspoons non-diet, tub-style margarine
⅓   cup of 1½-in.-long matchstick carrot strips
⅓   cup of 1½-in.-long matchstick celery strips
1   large garlic clove, minced
4   green onions, including tops, cut into matchstick strips
1   large bay leaf
10   saffron threads, very finely crumbled
     Pinch (generous) cayenne pepper
¼   cup fresh or canned tomatoes, peeled, seeded, and finely chopped
     Finely chopped fresh chives or parsley for garnish

To clean mussels, first rinse and drain them. Discard shells that are extremely lightweight (or empty!). Wash mussels in several changes of water, scrubbing shells with a vegetable brush. Continue changing water until it is clear and no traces of sand remain. Debeard mussels (trim off dark root-like particles), using kitchen shears or a sharp knife. Soak mussels in cold water, to just cover, for 2 or 3 hours or overnight to allow them to disgorge sand. (Alternatively, soak mussels in cold water sprinkled with a handful of cornmeal for about 1 hour.) Place mussels in colander. Discard any "gapers" that have not closed up. Wash mussels well under cold running water and set aside to drain.

Combine clam juice, water, and wine in large pot. Cover and bring mixture to a boil over high heat. Add mussels; re-cover pot. Steam mussels, shaking pot several times to redistribute them, for 5 minutes or until shells open. Remove pot from heat; let stand 5 minutes. Carefully drain off and reserve mussel cooking liquid. Discard unopened mussels.

In a 2- or 3-quart saucepan, melt margarine over medium heat. Stir in carrot, celery, and garlic and cook, stirring, 5 minutes; add tablespoon of water if needed to prevent vegetables from burning. Add green onions and cook, stirring, 2 minutes longer.

Using a slotted spoon, transfer vegetables from saucepan and reserve them in a small bowl. Using a fine sieve lined with several thicknesses of dampened cheesecloth, strain mussel cooking liquid into saucepan previously used. Add bay leaf, saffron, and cayenne pepper. Bring mixture to a boil over medium-high heat. Then, lower heat and simmer, covered, 10 minutes. Meanwhile, remove mussels from their shells and reserve them.

Return vegetables to pan and continue simmering 2 to 3 minutes or until carrots are just cooked through. Stir in tomatoes and reserved mussels and simmer 2 minutes longer. Discard bay leaf. Serve soup immediately, dividing mussels among soup plates or shallow bowls. Garnish servings with chopped chives or parsley.

Number of Servings: 5 (data per serving)

calories:	150	protein (gm):	16.1
% calories from fat:	23	fat (gm):	3.8
cholesterol (mg):	57	sodium (mg):	341

PORTUGUESE-STYLE FISHERMAN'S POT

◆

We prefer to use cultured mussels for soup making because they are usually cleaner and less likely to contain grit. Uncultured mussels can be substituted if washed well.
This is a robust, attractive, well-seasoned soup. It makes a festive meal-in-a-bowl.

◆

Makes 5 or 6 Servings.

20 to 24	fresh mussels, preferably cultured (see discussion under Mussel Soup with Saffron)
1	tablespoon olive oil, preferably extra-virgin
2	large onions, finely chopped
1	large carrot, finely chopped
1	small celery stalk, finely chopped
½	cup sweet red pepper, diced (if unavailable, substitute sweet green pepper)
¼	cup fresh parsley leaves, finely chopped
1	large garlic clove, minced
1½	cups chicken stock (pg. 195), *or* broth (defatted)
3 to 4	medium-sized boiling potatoes, peeled and cut into ½-in. cubes
1	35-oz. can peeled Italian (plum) tomatoes, including juice
¾	cup dry white wine
1	teaspoon sugar
1	large bay leaf
1¾	teaspoons paprika, preferably imported sweet paprika
1¾	teaspoons chili powder
¼	teaspoon celery seed
¼	teaspoon black pepper, preferably freshly ground
¼	teaspoon dried thyme leaves
	Pinch of saffron threads, very finely crumbled (optional)
	Pinch (generous) dried, crushed (hot) red pepper

Salt to taste

1½ lbs. fresh or frozen and thawed, boneless, skinless cod, haddock, or similar lean white fish fillets

½ lb. fresh or frozen and thawed medium-sized shrimp, peeled

Finely chopped fresh parsley leaves for garnish

Clean mussels as follows: First, rinse and drain. Wash in several changes of water, scrubbing shells with vegetable brush. Debeard mussels (trim off dark root-like debris), using kitchen shears or sharp knife. Continue changing water until it is clear and no traces of sand remain. Then soak mussels in cold water, to just cover, for 2 or 3 hours to allow them to disgorge any more sand. (Alternatively, soak mussels in cold water sprinkled with handful of cornmeal for about 1 hour.)

To complete preparations, combine oil, onions, carrot, celery, sweet pepper, parsley, and garlic in 5-quart or larger pot over medium heat. Cook, stirring, 4 to 5 minutes or until onions are limp; add a tablespoon or two of chicken stock as needed to prevent vegetables from burning.

Stir in remaining chicken stock and potatoes and bring mixture to a boil. Lower heat and simmer, covered, 12 to 15 minutes or until potatoes are just cooked through; stir occasionally to prevent potatoes from sticking to pot bottom. Add tomatoes, breaking them up with a spoon. Stir in wine, sugar, bay leaf, paprika, chili powder, celery seed, black pepper, thyme, saffron (if used), and red pepper. Cover pot and simmer, covered, 20 to 25 minutes until mixture is slightly thickened and flavors have mingled.

Meanwhile, turn out mussels into a colander. Rinse them well under cold running water. Discard mussels that are not tightly closed. Set the rest aside to drain. Cut any large fish fillets into quarters; cut small fillets in half and set aside. Add salt to stock if desired.

Add mussels and fish and simmer 4 minutes. Stir in shrimp and continue simmering, covered, until mussels open, fish pieces are cooked through but hold their shape, and shrimp turn pink and curl, about 4 to 6 minutes longer. Discard any mussels that have not opened.

Ladle soup into soup plates or large bowls and garnish each with sprinkling of chopped parsley. Furnish some extra bowls for discarding mussel shells.

Number of Servings: 6 *(data per serving)*

calories:	355	protein (gm):	40.0
% calories from fat:	16	fat (gm):	6.5
cholesterol (mg):	141	sodium (mg):	938

BERMUDA FISH CHOWDER

Like Manhattan-style chowders, Bermuda chowders typically contain tomatoes. However, they have a wonderful flavor and robustness all their own. The following recipe makes a very savory, not to mention economical, one-pot meal. It is excellent reheated. The chowder may be prepared with a quart of fresh or frozen (thawed) fish stock (see Index), or with 2 cups of bottled clam juice and 2 cups of chicken broth.
Traditionally in Bermuda, a bottle of sherry peppers is passed at the table to garnish the chowder. (Sherry peppers are very small, hot peppers steeped in dry sherry until their flavor and fire permeate the liquid.) Only the liquid is actually used on the chowder. In place of sherry peppers, you can top the chowder with a light sprinkling of dry sherry, and pass a bottle of Tabasco sauce. Or, simply omit the additions; the chowder is delicious as is!

Makes 5 to 7 Servings.

1 tablespoon canola, safflower, or corn oil
2 large onions, finely chopped
4 medium-sized celery stalks, including leaves, chopped
4 cups fish stock (pg. 201), *or* 2 cups bottled clam juice and 2 cups chicken broth (defatted)
4 medium-sized carrots, chopped
½ medium-sized sweet green pepper, chopped
2½ teaspoons Worcestershire sauce
2 large bay leaves
½ teaspoon dried thyme
¼ teaspoon black pepper
1 teaspoon mild curry powder
2 small ham hocks (about 1 lb.)
3¼ cups ½-in. peeled boiling potato cubes
1½ cups canned chopped Italian-style tomatoes, including juice
⅓ cup ketchup
½ teaspoon salt, or to taste
1 lb. fresh or frozen and thawed lean, boneless, skinless, white fish fillets (flounder, haddock, cod, etc.), cut into 1-in. chunks

Bermuda sherry peppers for garnish (or
substitute Tabasco sauce and teaspoon or two
of dry sherry), optional

I n a large pot over medium-high heat, combine oil, onion, and celery. Cook over medium heat, stirring, 5 to 6 minutes or until onion is limp; add tablespoon or two of stock if needed to prevent vegetables from burning during cooking.

Stir in carrots and green pepper and cook, stirring, 2 minutes longer. Stir in remainder of stock (or clam juice-chicken broth mixture), Worcestershire sauce, bay leaves, thyme, black pepper, curry powder, and ham hocks. Add potatoes and bring mixture to a boil over medium-high heat. Lower heat and simmer, covered, 20 minutes.

Stir in tomatoes and ketchup; re-cover pot and simmer 1½ hours longer. Stir in salt and fish and continue simmering, covered, about 30 minutes longer. Discard bay leaves and ham hocks.

Bermuda Fish Chowder is good reheated. Reheat over medium-high heat until piping hot. Thin chowder with a little water if desired.

Number of Servings: 7 *(data per serving)*

calories:	272	protein (gm):	27.3
% calories from fat:	21	fat (gm):	6.4
cholesterol (mg):	26	sodium (mg):	767

FRESH SALMON CHOWDER WITH POTATOES

◆

Normally, fresh poached salmon makes a very healthful but expensive meal. When incorporated into a mild, homey chowder, however, it is still delicious but also fairly economical to serve. North Atlantic salmon and Pacific king salmon are both good choices for this recipe.

◆

Makes 4 to 5 Servings.

3 cups fish stock (pg. 201), *or* bottled clam juice (if unavailable, substitute chicken broth), divided
8 ozs. fresh, boneless salmon fillet
1 tablespoon non-diet, tub-style margarine
1 cup onions, chopped
2 tablespoons celery with leaves, finely chopped
1 tablespoon all-purpose white flour
¼ teaspoon dry mustard
¼ teaspoon dried marjoram
3¼ cups boiling potatoes, peeled and cubed (½-in. cubes)
¼ teaspoon white pepper
1 cup whole milk*

I n a large pot, bring ¾ cup fish stock or clam juice to a simmer over medium-low heat. Add salmon fillets, skin side down. Lower heat and gently poach fish, covered, 5 to 8 minutes or until just cooked through (turns opaque) at thickest part and begins to flake. Immediately remove fish to a bowl, laying it skin side up. Strain poaching liquid through a fine sieve into the bowl.

Wipe out pot and add margarine, onions, and celery to it. Cook over medium-low heat, stirring frequently, until onions are limp, about 5 minutes. Stir in flour until incorporated. Cook, stirring, 1 minute. Stir in 1 cup of remaining stock until incorporated smoothly into flour. Add remaining stock, mustard, marjoram, potatoes, and pepper.

Bring mixture to a boil over medium-high heat. Lower heat and simmer, uncovered, about 12 minutes or until potatoes are tender. Meanwhile, when salmon is cool enough to handle, carefully peel off and discard skin. Using fork, flake salmon into bite-sized pieces.

Using a measuring cup, scoop up ½ cup vegetables and broth from pot and transfer to blender. Blend until completely pureed. Return puree and milk to pot. Add flaked salmon. Let mixture return to a simmer and serve immediately.

The chowder may also be refrigerated up to 48 hours and reheated.

Number of Servings: 5 *(data per serving)*

calories:	257	protein (gm):	18.1
% calories from fat:	25	fat (gm):	7.1
cholesterol (mg):	26	sodium (mg):	287

*Note: To lower fat in recipe even further, substitute 2% milk for whole milk.

WHITE CLAM CHOWDER WITH CORN

Very savory, hearty, and rich-tasting yet light on fat.

Makes 4 to 5 Servings.

- 1 tablespoon non-diet, tub-style margarine
- 1 medium-sized onion, chopped
- 1 large celery stalk, chopped
- 1 tablespoon all-purpose white flour
- 1 cup bottled clam juice, *or* substitute chicken broth (defatted)
- 1 10½-oz. can minced clams, including juice
- 1 large bay leaf
- ¼ teaspoon dried marjoram leaves
- ⅛ teaspoon (generous) black pepper, or to taste
- 2 cups boiling potatoes, peeled and cubed (¼-in. cubes)
- 2 cups frozen yellow corn kernels, rinsed under warm water and thoroughly drained
- 1 cup 2% milk
- Salt to taste

In a large pot, melt margarine over medium-high heat. Add onions and celery and cook, stirring, until onions are limp, about 5 minutes. Stir in flour until incorporated. Cook, stirring, 30 seconds. Stir in bottled clam juice, continuing to stir until mixture is well blended.

Add juice drained from the canned clams (reserve the minced clams for adding later), bay leaf, marjoram, pepper, and potatoes. Bring mixture to a boil. Reduce heat and simmer mixture, covered and stirring occasionally, 10 minutes. Add corn and continue simmering 5 minutes longer. Discard bay leaf.

Using a measuring cup, scoop up 1 cup vegetables and liquid from pot and transfer to blender or food processor. Blend or process until thoroughly pureed. Return puree to soup, along with the milk and minced clams. Bring chowder to a simmer and stir in salt if desired. Serve immediately.

The chowder may also be refrigerated up to 48 hours and reheated.

Number of Servings: 5 *(data per serving)*

calories:	205	protein (gm):	11.1
% calories from fat:	18	fat (gm):	4.1
cholesterol (mg):	41	sodium (mg):	153

MEAT
SOUPS

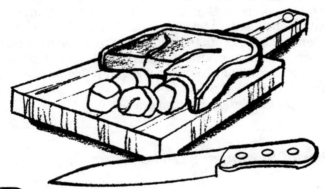

RED BEAN, RICE, AND
SAUSAGE SOUP

◆

*Turkey sausage gives this easy but satisfying soup its flavor.
The sausage retains its flavor best when it is added near the
end of the cooking time.*

◆

Makes 6 to 8 Servings.
1 large onion, finely chopped
1 large garlic clove, minced
1 teaspoon olive oil

3½ cups chicken broth (defatted), divided
1 large carrot, diced
1 large celery stalk, diced
½ sweet red pepper, diced (if unavailable,
    substitute sweet green pepper)
1½ cups water
1 15-oz. can reduced-sodium tomato sauce, *or*
    regular tomato sauce
4 cups cooked kidney beans, *or* 2 16-oz. cans
    dark red kidney beans, drained
¼ teaspoon (generous) dried thyme leaves
1 bay leaf
¼ teaspoon black pepper
⅓ cup long-grain white rice
6 ozs. smoked turkey sausage cut into ¼-in.
    slices

I n a Dutch oven or small soup pot, combine onion, garlic, olive oil, and 3 tablespoons chicken broth. Cook over medium heat, stirring frequently, until onions begin to brown, about 5 to 6 minutes. Add all remaining ingredients except sausage. Bring soup to a boil over high heat. Lower heat, cover, and simmer, stirring occasionally, about 20 minutes. Add sausage and cook an additional 10 minutes or until flavors are well blended and soup has thickened slightly.

This soup keeps 3 to 4 days in refrigerator.

Number of Servings: 8 *(data per serving)*

calories:	240	protein (gm):	16.3
% calories from fat:	16	fat (gm):	4.3
cholesterol (mg):	18	sodium (mg):	779

BEEFY MINESTRONE

There are many versions of this popular Italian vegetable-pasta soup. This one is somewhat Americanized, as it substitutes beef for the more traditional salt pork. The soup tastes wonderful reheated and should be made the day before needed so that the fat can be easily removed. (The pasta and tomatoes are added after reheating.)

Makes 9 to 10 Servings.

4 to 5   lbs. beef soup bones
   1   large onion, coarsely chopped
   1   large garlic clove, minced
  10   cups water
   ½   cup dry Great Northern beans, picked over and rinsed
   2   large celery stalks, including leaves, diced
   2   medium-sized carrots, thinly sliced
   2   cups green cabbage, coarsely shredded
   2   cups zucchini, coarsely diced
   1   lb. beef round, cut into small bite-sized pieces
   ½   cup fresh parsley leaves, chopped
   3   bay leaves
   4   beef bouillon cubes
  1½   teaspoons dried basil leaves
  1½   teaspoons dried oregano leaves
   ½   teaspoon dried thyme leaves
   ½   teaspoon black pepper
   1   14½- to 16-oz. can tomatoes (preferably Italian plum tomatoes), including juice
   1   15-oz. can reduced-sodium tomato sauce, *or* regular tomato sauce
   1   cup small elbow macaroni or other pasta shapes, uncooked
       Salt to taste

I n a large, heavy pot, combine bones, onion, garlic, and water. Add beans, celery, carrots, and cabbage. Bring mixture to a boil over high heat. Cover, lower heat, and simmer 1 hour. Add zucchini, beef cubes, parsley, bay leaves, bouillon cubes, basil, oregano, thyme, and pepper.

Simmer an additional 1 hour to 1¼ hours, stirring occasionally, or until beans are tender. Remove and discard bones and bay leaves.

Refrigerate soup overnight. Remove solidified fat from top of soup and discard. Add tomatoes and tomato sauce, breaking tomatoes up with a spoon. Carefully reheat soup over low to medium heat, stirring to prevent burning.

Re-cover pot and bring soup to a boil. Add pasta. Simmer an additional 14 to 17 minutes, stirring frequently, or until pasta is tender and flavors are well blended. Add salt if desired.

After refrigeration, the pasta tends to thicken the soup. During reheating, you may want to thin soup with a small amount of water or beef bouillon.

Number of Servings: 10 *(data per serving)*

calories:	217	protein (gm):	19.9
% calories from fat:	21	fat (gm):	5.0
cholesterol (mg):	28	sodium (mg):	463

BEEF AND BARLEY SOUP

Rich and thick, this beef soup is a meal in a bowl. After the bones have flavored the soup and before most of the vegetables are added, we recommend refrigerating the soup so that the solidified fat can be removed. (Or, if you're in a hurry, you could carefully skim off and discard the fat before adding the vegetables.)

Makes 8 to 9 Servings.

4 lbs. beef soup bones
10 cups water
2 celery stalks, including leaves, thinly sliced
2 medium-sized carrots, thinly sliced
1 large Spanish onion, finely chopped
1 lb. beef round, well trimmed and cut into ¾-in. cubes
½ cup pearl barley
3 bay leaves
2 garlic cloves, minced
4 beef bouillon cubes
1 15-oz. can reduced-sodium tomato sauce, *or* regular tomato sauce
½ cup fresh parsley leaves, finely chopped
3 medium-sized potatoes, peeled and cut into ¾-in. cubes
2 cups fresh or frozen green beans
2 cups cabbage, thinly sliced
2 teaspoons dried thyme leaves
2 teaspoons sugar
¾ teaspoon dried marjoram leaves
¾ teaspoon dried basil leaves
½ teaspoon chili powder
¼ teaspoon ground celery seed
½ teaspoon black pepper
Salt to taste

I n a large, heavy pot, combine bones, water, celery, carrots, onion, beef round, barley, bay leaves, garlic, and bouillon cubes and bring mixture to a boil over high heat. Cover, lower heat, and simmer, stirring occasionally, about 1 hour and 40 minutes. With a slotted spoon, remove bones from pot and discard. Remove bay leaves and discard. To remove fat, soup should be refrigerated for 6 or 7 hours or overnight at this point and completed later.

With a large, shallow spoon, remove solidified fat from top of soup and discard. Carefully reheat soup over low to medium heat, stirring to prevent sticking. If soup seems too thick, add a bit more water. Bring soup to a boil.

Add tomato sauce, parsley, potatoes, green beans, cabbage, thyme, sugar, marjoram, basil, chili powder, celery seed, and black pepper. Re-cover, lower heat, and simmer soup an additional 30 to 40 minutes or until potatoes are tender. Add salt if desired.

This soup keeps 4 to 5 days in refrigerator.

Number of Servings: 9 *(data per serving)*

calories:	241	protein (gm):	20.3
% calories from fat:	19	fat (gm):	5.1
cholesterol (mg):	31	sodium (mg):	442

SPICY BEEF AND CABBAGE SOUP

The combination of cabbage, vinegar, sugar, and spices gives this easy soup its zip. If you like, substitute the more nutritious brown rice for the white, and add the rice along with the bouillon.

Makes 6 to 8 Servings.

¾ lb. ground beef round*
1 large onion, finely chopped
1 large garlic clove, minced
4 cups beef bouillon, reconstituted from cubes
3 cups water
2 celery stalks, including leaves, thinly sliced
2 large carrots, thinly sliced
3 bay leaves
1 15-oz. can reduced-sodium tomato sauce, *or* regular tomato sauce
3 cups cabbage, grated or very finely shredded
½ teaspoon powdered mustard
2 tablespoons apple cider vinegar
2 tablespoons sugar
½ teaspoon dried thyme leaves
½ teaspoon dried marjoram leaves
¼ teaspoon ground cinnamon
⅛ teaspoon ground cloves
½ teaspoon black pepper
⅓ cup white rice, uncooked
Salt to taste

I n a large, heavy soup pot, combine ground round, onion, and garlic. Cook over medium heat, stirring frequently, until meat is browned. Remove pot from heat. Turn meat and onion mixture out onto a large plate covered with paper towels. When paper towels have absorbed the fat, return meat mixture to pot.

Add all remaining ingredients except rice. Bring to a boil over high heat and simmer, covered, 15 minutes. Add rice. Lower heat, cover, and simmer about 40 minutes or until cabbage and rice are cooked and flavors are well blended. Add salt if desired. Skim off and discard remaining fat from top of soup.

This soup keeps 4 to 5 days in refrigerator.

Number of Servings: 8 (data per serving)

calories:	154	protein (gm):	10.2
% calories from fat:	24	fat (gm):	4.1
cholesterol (mg):	25	sodium (mg):	490

*Note: To reduce fat, decrease meat to ½ lb.

CORN AND BEAN CON CARNE SOUP

Ground beef is an excellent soup ingredient. A relatively small amount per serving adds satisfying flavor and texture to a whole pot of broth and vegetables.

Makes 6 to 8 Servings.

¾ lb. ground beef round*

1 large onion, finely chopped

1 garlic clove, minced

4 cups beef bouillon reconstituted from cubes

2 cups reduced-sodium tomato juice, *or* regular tomato juice

1 16-oz. can reduced-sodium tomatoes, including juice, *or* regular tomatoes

4 cups cooked kidney beans, *or* 2 15½-oz. cans kidney beans, well drained

2 cups frozen corn kernels

¼ 4-oz. can chopped green chilies, rinsed and drained

1 large carrot, chopped

2 teaspoons chili powder, or to taste

2 teaspoons sugar

½ teaspoon ground cumin

¼ teaspoon black pepper

⅓ cup white rice, uncooked

Salt to taste

In a large pot, combine ground round, onion, and garlic. Cook over medium heat, stirring frequently and breaking meat up with large spoon, 5 or 6 minutes or until browned. If meat sticks to pan, add a small amount of beef bouillon.

Add remaining bouillon, tomato juice, and tomatoes, breaking up tomatoes with large spoon. Stir in kidney beans, corn, and chilies. Add all remaining ingredients, *except* rice, and stir to mix well.

Bring soup to a boil. Cover pan, lower heat, and simmer soup 15 minutes. Bring soup to a boil again. Stir in rice. Lower heat and simmer an additional half-hour or until rice is cooked and flavors are well blended.

Add salt if desired. With a large, shallow spoon, skim off and discard fat from top of soup.

This soup keeps 4 to 5 days in refrigerator.

Number of Servings: 8 *(data per serving)*

calories:	294	protein (gm):	18.5
% calories from fat:	17	fat (gm):	5.7
cholesterol (mg):	25	sodium (mg):	534

*Note: To reduce fat, decrease meat to ½ lb.

MEATBALL AND VEGETABLE SOUP

Browning the meatballs in the oven makes preparation easier, eliminates the need for extra fat, and actually removes fat from the meat.

Makes 6 to 8 Servings.

Soup

- 1 medium-sized onion, finely chopped
- 1 garlic clove, minced
- 2 celery stalks, diced
- 1 16-oz. can reduced-sodium tomatoes, *or* regular tomatoes pureed in food processor or blender
- 4 cups canned beef broth (defatted), *or* 4 cups beef bouillon reconstituted from 4 bouillon cubes
- 2 cups water
- 1 8-oz. can tomato sauce
- 2 large carrots, thinly sliced
- 2 cups frozen corn kernels
- 2 cups 1-in. fresh green bean pieces, *or* 2 cups frozen green beans
- 2 cups fresh cauliflower, coarsely chopped
- ¼ cup pearl barley
- 2 bay leaves
- 2 teaspoons sugar
- 1 teaspoon dried basil leaves
- ½ teaspoon dried thyme leaves
- ½ teaspoon powdered mustard
- ½ teaspoon chili powder
  Dash (generous) ground cloves
- ¼ teaspoon black pepper
  Salt to taste

Meatballs

- ¾ lb. ground round of beef
- 2 teaspoons instant minced onions

1 large egg white
¼ cup rolled oats, uncooked
2 tablespoons ketchup
⅛ teaspoon dried thyme leaves
⅛ teaspoon powdered mustard
¼ teaspoon salt
⅛ teaspoon black pepper

I n a large soup pot over medium heat, combine onion, garlic, celery, and pureed tomatoes. Simmer gently 5 or 6 minutes, until onion is tender. Add all remaining soup ingredients, and stir to mix well. Bring soup to a boil. Cover pot, lower heat, and simmer about 1 hour and 20 minutes.

Meanwhile, combine all meatball ingredients in a medium-sized bowl, and mix them together well. Form meat mixture into about 24 balls, using a scant tablespoon of mixture for each. Place meatballs on rimmed baking sheet or jelly roll pan, and bake in preheated 350-degree oven 10 to 13 minutes or until nicely browned. Remove meatballs with slotted spoon, and transfer them to soup pot so that they cook for at least 25 to 30 minutes.

When soup is cooked, skim fat from top of liquid with large, shallow spoon and discard. Add salt if desired. Remove bay leaves and discard.

This soup keeps 2 to 3 days in refrigerator.

Number of Servings: 8 (data per serving)

calories:	210	protein (gm):	14.0
% calories from fat:	21	fat (gm):	4.8
cholesterol (mg):	25	sodium (mg):	557

LAMB AND WHITE BEAN SOUP

If you like bean soup, try this version with lamb shanks. For best flavor, the bones should be cracked before cooking. When you buy the shanks, ask the butcher to do this. This soup tastes best when refrigerated overnight and reheated. Also, chilling is important to remove the fat.

Makes 7 to 8 Servings.

- 1½ cups dry Great Northern or navy beans, sorted and washed
- 2 lamb shanks (about 1¾ lbs. total)
- 6 cups beef bouillon reconstituted from cubes
- 2 cups water
- 2 large carrots, sliced
- 2 large celery stalks, sliced
- 1 large onion, very finely chopped
- 2 large garlic cloves, minced
- 3 bay leaves
- 1½ teaspoons dried thyme leaves
- 1¼ teaspoons dried marjoram leaves
- ½ teaspoon (scant) ground celery seed
- ½ teaspoon powdered mustard
- ¼ teaspoon black pepper
- 3 cups cabbage, thinly sliced
- Salt to taste

Put beans in a large, heavy pot and cover with about 2 in. of cold water. Bring to a boil over high heat. Cover, lower heat, and simmer 2 minutes. Remove pot from heat and let stand at room temperature for 1 hour. Drain beans in a colander and discard the soaking water.

Return beans to pot in which they were cooked. Add all remaining ingredients *except* cabbage and salt. Bring to a boil, lower heat, and simmer 1 hour. Add cabbage and simmer an additional 30 to 40 minutes until beans are very tender.

Remove and discard bay leaves. With slotted spoon, remove bones and meat to a medium-sized bowl. When shanks are cool enough to handle, cut lean meat into bite-sized pieces and return them to pot.

Refrigerate soup overnight. Before serving, use a large, shallow spoon to remove solidified fat from top of pot. A few shreds of cabbage will come

away with the fat and can be discarded, too. Reheat soup carefully over medium heat, stirring constantly to prevent burning. Add salt if desired.
This soup keeps 4 to 5 days in refrigerator.

Number of Servings: 8 *(data per serving)*

calories:	180	protein (gm):	17.0
% calories from fat:	17	fat (gm):	3.4
cholesterol (mg):	31	sodium (mg):	697

HAM AND SPLIT PEA SOUP

Thick and satisfying, this soup is a meal in a bowl. Make it when you have a leftover ham bone from a party or holiday dinner. Or purchase a bone from a specialty shop. If you prefer the soup without meat, you can use 2 large ham hocks in place of the ham bone. Discard the ham hocks when the soup has finished cooking. Since the flavor may not be as rich with ham hocks, you may need to use additional bouillon.

Makes 7 to 9 Servings.

2 large garlic cloves, minced
2 large onions, finely chopped
9 cups water
1 meaty ham bone (or 2 large ham hocks)
2 cups (1 lb.) dried green split peas, picked over and rinsed
2 beef bouillon cubes (or more if needed)
2 bay leaves
2 large carrots, thinly sliced
¼ cup fresh parsley leaves, finely chopped
2 large celery stalks, including leaves, thinly sliced
½ teaspoon dried thyme leaves
½ teaspoon dried marjoram leaves
½ teaspoon celery salt
½ teaspoon black pepper
   Salt to taste

I n a large soup pot, combine all ingredients except salt. Bring to a boil over high heat. Cover and lower heat. Simmer, stirring occasionally, until split peas have cooked completely and thickened the soup, about 1½ to 1¾ hours. As soup thickens, stir more frequently and lower heat to prevent split peas from sticking to bottom of pot. Add additional bouillon if needed.

Remove ham bone. While meat on the bone is cooling slightly, skim fat off top of soup with large, shallow spoon, and discard. Remove bay leaves and discard. Then cut meat into small pieces and return it to soup. Add salt if desired. Bring soup to a boil again. Stir well before serving.

This soup tastes wonderful reheated. However, it must be stirred carefully to prevent the split peas from sticking. If it thickens too much in refrigerator, thin with a bit more water during reheating.

This soup keeps 4 to 5 days in refrigerator.

◆

Number of Servings: 9 *(data per serving)*

calories:	149	protein (gm):	10.5
% calories from fat:	12	fat (gm):	2.0
cholesterol (mg):	4	sodium (mg):	409

HEARTY SPLIT PEA, BEAN, AND BARLEY SOUP

We love split pea soup. But we love this stick-to-the-ribs variation even more for its pleasing variety of textures. The combination of split peas, beans, black-eyed peas, and barley complements the flavor of the smoked meat perfectly. (Or you can substitute baby lima beans for the black-eyed peas or navy beans.) This version feeds a crowd, and it's a perfect way to use a leftover ham bone. A bone can also be purchased at shops that specialize in sliced ham. Smoked pork hocks can also be used in place of the ham bone, although the flavor will be less intense. The number of beef bouillon cubes needed in the recipe will vary, depending on the size of the ham bone used, the amount of meat attached, and whether pork hocks are substituted.

Makes 12 to 14 Servings.

15 cups water
1 meaty ham bone, *or* 2 large pork hocks (about 2 lbs. total)
2 cups (1 lb.) dry green split peas, picked over and rinsed
½ cup pearl barley
½ cup dry black-eyed peas, picked over and rinsed
½ cup dry navy beans, picked over and rinsed
3 bay leaves
2 beef bouillon cubes (or up to 5, as needed)
2 large onions, coarsely chopped
2 large carrots, thinly sliced
2 large celery stalks, including leaves, thinly sliced
2 garlic cloves, minced
½ teaspoon (generous) dried thyme leaves
½ teaspoon ground celery seed
½ teaspoon black pepper
  Salt to taste

I n a large, heavy soup pot, combine water, ham bone, split peas, barley, black-eyed peas, and beans. Bring to a boil over high heat. Add bay leaves, 2 bouillon cubes, onions, carrots, celery, garlic, thyme, celery seed, and pepper. Cover and lower heat. Simmer, stirring occasionally, until beans are tender and split peas have thickened the soup, about 2 to 2½ hours.

As soup thickens, lower heat and stir more frequently to prevent split peas from sticking to bottom of pot. Taste the soup. If more bouillon cubes are needed, add them, along with salt if desired. When beans are tender, remove ham bone or pork hocks. If pork hocks have been used, discard them. If a ham bone has been used, reserve and cool slightly.

Meanwhile, remove soup from heat and skim fat off top with large, shallow spoon, and discard. Then, if a ham bone has been used, cut meat into bite-sized pieces and return it to soup. Bring soup to a boil again. Stir well before serving.

This soup tastes wonderful reheated. However, it must be stirred carefully to prevent split peas from sticking. If it thickens too much in refrigerator, thin with a bit more water during reheating.

This soup keeps 4 to 5 days in refrigerator.

Number of Servings: 14   (data per serving)

calories:	150	protein (gm):	9.3
% calories from fat:	6	fat (gm):	1.0
cholesterol (mg):	2	sodium (mg):	198

CHINESE PORK AND WATERCRESS SOUP

In this recipe the watercress is barely cooked at all, which helps retain its bright color and fresh, peppery taste.

Makes 5 to 6 Servings.

2½ ozs. fresh pork loin, well trimmed and cut into very thin 1-in.-long strips

1 small garlic clove, halved

¼ in.-thick slice fresh ginger root, peeled

5½ cups chicken stock (pg. 195), *or* broth (defatted), divided

4 to 5 scallions, including 1 in. of green top, quartered lengthwise and cut into 1-in. lengths

1 tablespoon dry sherry

1 teaspoon reduced-salt soy sauce

⅔ cup cooked white rice

1½ cups (lightly packed) fresh, tender watercress sprigs

C ombine pork strips, garlic clove halves, and ginger root in small saucepan. Add ½ cup of stock and bring mixture to a simmer over medium-high heat. Simmer, covered, 6 to 7 minutes or until pork is cooked through. Remove pan from heat.

Using a slotted spoon, transfer pork strips to a colander. Rinse pork thoroughly under cool water to remove any froth; set aside to drain. Strain broth used to cook pork through a very fine sieve into a 2- to 3-quart saucepan; discard garlic and ginger root.

Add the remaining 5 cups of stock, scallions, sherry, soy sauce, and rice to sieved broth. Bring mixture to a boil. Then lower heat and simmer, covered, 2 minutes.

Stir in watercress. Remove pan from heat and let stand 30 seconds or until watercress is wilted but not cooked. Serve immediately.

Number of Servings: 6 *(data per serving)*

calories:	83	protein (gm):	7.9
% calories from fat:	17	fat (gm):	1.6
cholesterol (mg):	8	sodium (mg):	439

SOUTHERN-STYLE SOUP WITH GREENS

This is savory, substantial, and good.

Makes 4 to 5 Servings.

⅔ lb. fresh, crisp, collard greens

2 teaspoons canola, safflower, or corn oil

2 medium-sized onions, coarsely chopped

4 cups chicken stock (pg. 195), *or* broth (defatted)

2½ cups water

2 small ham hocks (about 1¼ lbs.)

4 medium-sized carrots, cut into ¼-in. slices

1 large bay leaf

¼ teaspoon dried thyme

¼ teaspoon black pepper, preferably freshly ground

4½ cups thin-skinned potatoes, unpeeled and very coarsely cubed (if unavailable, substitute regular, peeled boiling potatoes)

½ cup very lean, cooked ham, diced

Thoroughly wash collards and drain in colander. Cut or tear leaves from stems and tough midribs; discard stems and midribs. Tear leaves into small bite-sized pieces. To remove all traces of grit, thoroughly wash collard leaves again; then set aside to drain.

Combine oil and onions in 4-quart or larger soup pot or saucepan. Cook onions over medium heat, stirring, 5 to 6 minutes or until very limp but not browned. Add chicken stock, water, and ham hocks and bring pot to a boil. Add collards and cook, stirring, until they wilt slightly. Stir in carrots, bay leaf, thyme, and pepper.

Allow pot to return to a boil. Cover pot, lower heat, and simmer mixture 10 minutes. Stir in potatoes and ham and continue cooking soup, covered, 25 to 30 minutes longer or until collards are tender. (The larger and more mature the collard leaves, the longer they will take.)

Remove bay leaf and ham hocks from pot and discard. Skim off fat from soup surface, using large, shallow spoon and serve.

Keeps, refrigerated, 3 or 4 days.

Number of Servings: 5 *(data per serving)*

calories:	254	protein (gm):	15.9
% calories from fat:	24	fat (gm):	6.8
cholesterol (mg):	33	sodium (mg):	573

EASY BARBECUED BEEF AND VEGETABLE SOUP

Makes 6 to 7 Servings.

- 1 lb. lean beef round, well-trimmed and cut into ½-in. cubes
- 1 tablespoon canola, safflower, or corn oil
- 3 large onions, coarsely chopped
- 3 cups beef stock (pg. 199), *or* broth (defatted)
- ½ cup water
- 1 cup rutabaga or turnip, peeled and diced
- 1 cup celery, coarsely chopped
- 1 tablespoon chili powder
- ¾ teaspoon dried thyme leaves
- ¾ teaspoon dry mustard
- ¾ teaspoon ground allspice
- ¼ teaspoon black pepper
- 4 cups potatoes, peeled and cubed (½-in. cubes)
- 2 cups carrots, peeled and sliced (⅛-in.-thick slices)
- 1 cup 1-in. fresh or frozen cut green bean pieces
- 1 15-oz. can tomato sauce
- 2½ tablespoons packed light or dark brown sugar
- 1 tablespoon apple cider vinegar
  Salt to taste

Combine beef and oil in 6-quart soup pot over medium-high heat. Cook beef, stirring, 4 to 5 minutes or until lightly browned. Add onions and cook, stirring, several minutes longer, until onion is limp. Add stock, water, rutabaga, celery, chili powder, thyme, mustard, allspice, and pepper. Bring to a boil over high heat. Lower heat, cover pot, and simmer mixture 20 minutes.

Add potatoes, carrots, and green beans and let mixture return to a simmer. Continue simmering 30 to 40 minutes longer or until carrots, potatoes, and beef are tender.

Stir tomato sauce, brown sugar, and vinegar together in a bowl until sugar dissolves. Add tomato sauce mixture and continue simmering soup about 15 minutes longer. Add salt if desired. Skim fat from soup surface, using a large, shallow spoon.

Serve immediately, or refrigerate up to 3 days before serving.

Number of Servings: 7 *(data per serving)*

calories:	253	protein (gm):	17.8
% calories from fat:	25	fat (gm):	7.1
cholesterol (mg):	39	sodium (mg):	622

LENTIL-BARLEY SOUP WITH BEEF

◆

Very hearty, healthful, and economical, this soup features a savory blend of lentils, rice, barley, corn, and beef.

Makes 5 to 7 Servings.

3 lbs. beef neck bones, preferably very meaty
2 cups water
5 cups beef stock (pg. 199), *or* broth (defatted), *or* beef bouillon reconstituted from cubes or granules
3 medium-sized onions, finely chopped
3 large celery stalks, finely chopped
⅓ cup fresh parsley, chopped
¼ cup dry lentils, sorted and washed
¼ cup pearl barley
2 tablespoons long-grain brown rice, uncooked
1 teaspoon dried thyme leaves
⅛ teaspoon ground allspice
¼ teaspoon (generous) black pepper
2 large carrots, diced
1 medium-sized turnip, diced
1 cup frozen yellow corn kernels
  Salt to taste

P reheat oven to 400 degrees. Rinse and drain bones well. Pat dry with paper towels. Spread bones in large roasting pan. Roast 30 minutes, stirring occasionally to ensure even browning and to prevent burning. Pour off and discard any fat released into pan. Roast bones 30 to 40 minutes longer, stirring occasionally.

Transfer contents of roasting pan to large soup pot or stock pot. Pour water into roasting pan. Using a wooden spoon, scrape up any browned bits sticking to bottom. Transfer water and browned bits to stock pot. Add beef stock, onions, celery, and parsley. Bring mixture to a boil over high heat. Cover pot and adjust heat so mixture gently simmers 45 minutes.

Stir in lentils, barley, rice, thyme, allspice, pepper, carrots, and turnip and continue simmering, covered, 1 hour longer. Remove bones from pot and set them aside to cool. Very carefully skim off and discard fat from soup surface, using large, shallow spoon. (Or to defat soup more efficiently, wait until soup finishes cooking; refrigerate it several hours until fat solidifies on surface, and then lift off and discard fat.) Stir corn and salt (if desired) into soup and simmer about 10 minutes longer.

When meat is cool enough to handle, remove it from bones and return it to pot. Reheat briefly and serve. Or serve soup reheated; thin with a little beef broth or water during heating if necessary.

Number of Servings: 7 (data per serving)

calories:	196	protein (gm):	17.0
% calories from fat:	21	fat (gm):	4.5
cholesterol (mg):	33	sodium (mg):	377

SPICY LENTIL-TOMATO SOUP WITH HAM

◆

This easy, spicy lentil soup is seasoned with ham, tomatoes, and a lively blend of herbs.

◆

Makes 6 to 7 Servings.

1 tablespoon olive oil, preferably extra-virgin
3 cups onions, chopped
2 large garlic cloves, minced
4 cups chicken stock (pg. 195), *or* broth (defatted)
2 cups water
2 ham hocks (about 1 lb.)
1 cup celery with leaves, finely chopped
1 cup carrots, finely diced
½ cup red lentils or regular lentils, rinsed and drained
1 tablespoon dried basil leaves
½ teaspoon dried oregano leaves
½ teaspoon dried thyme leaves
⅛ teaspoon (scant) ground cayenne pepper
⅛ teaspoon black pepper, or to taste
½ cup very lean ham, finely diced
1 28-oz. can Italian-style tomatoes (including juice), coarsely chopped
1 cup green cabbage, shredded
1 cup cooked garbanzo beans, *or* canned garbanzo beans, rinsed and drained

C ombine olive oil, onions, and garlic in large pot. Cook over medium heat, stirring frequently, until onions are limp and most liquid has evaporated from pot, about 5 minutes. Add stock, water, ham hocks, celery, carrots, lentils, basil, oregano, thyme, cayenne pepper, and black pepper. Bring mixture to a boil over medium-high heat. Lower heat and simmer, covered, about 45 minutes.

Using a large, shallow spoon, skim off fat from soup surface. Discard ham hocks. Add diced ham, tomatoes, cabbage, and garbanzo beans and simmer 15 minutes longer.

This soup may be refrigerated up to 3 days or frozen and reheated over low heat if desired. Stir frequently during reheating to prevent soup from sticking to bottom of pot.

Number of Servings: 7 *(data per serving)*

calories:	213	protein (gm):	15.6
% calories from fat:	27	fat (gm):	6.4
cholesterol (mg):	28	sodium (mg):	792

BEAN, GRAIN, AND PASTA SOUPS

Although many of the soups in this chapter are cooked in chicken or
beef broth, and others get their flavor from pork hocks, none actually has any meat. However, these are some of the heartiest and most satisfying soups we know. Many of these full-bodied dishes, such as Garbanzo
and Couscous Soup; Hearty Split Pea, Bean, and Barley Soup; and Chili
Lentil Corn Soup, feature interesting grain and bean combinations.

But their calorie content is relatively modest. Beans and grains are
high in complex carbohydrates and low in fat. They fill you up without
filling you out. They also combine in these soups to provide high quality
protein. And they're very easy on the budget.

Incidentally, while we usually recommend that dry beans be covered
with water, brought to a boil, and soaked an hour before cooking, this procedure isn't absolutely necessary. Soaking makes beans more digestible and
helps them cook more evenly. But if you're in a hurry, you can omit the
step. Depending on the variety, beans will need to simmer 15 to 30 minutes
longer if they were not soaked beforehand. Stir them several times to
ensure even cooking.

White Bean And Angel Hair Pasta Soup

Makes 6 to 8 Servings.

1½ cups dry Great Northern beans, washed and sorted
2 teaspoons olive oil
1 large onion, chopped
2 garlic cloves, chopped
7 cups chicken bouillon, reconstituted from cubes or granules, divided
1 cup water
1 pork hock (about ½ lb.)
2 large carrots, sliced
2 large celery stalks, including leaves, sliced
½ cup fresh parsley leaves, chopped
2 large bay leaves
1½ teaspoons dried basil leaves
1 teaspoon dried marjoram leaves
½ teaspoon dried thyme leaves
½ teaspoon dried oregano leaves
  Dash (generous) cayenne pepper
¼ teaspoon black pepper
2½ ozs. angel hair pasta, uncooked, broken in pieces (about 2¼ cups)
1 8-oz. can reduced-sodium tomato sauce, *or* regular tomato sauce
  Salt to taste

Place beans in large Dutch oven or soup pot. Cover with 2 in. water and bring to a boil over high heat. Lower heat and boil 2 minutes. Remove pot from heat, cover, and let beans stand 1 hour. Drain beans in a colander, discarding soaking water.

In the pot in which beans were cooked, combine olive oil, onion, garlic, and 3 tablespoons of bouillon. Cook onion and garlic over medium heat, stirring frequently, 5 or 6 minutes or until onion is soft. If liquid begins to evaporate, add a bit more bouillon. Add remaining bouillon.

Return beans to pot. Add water, pork hock, carrots, celery, parsley, bay leaves, basil, marjoram, thyme, oregano, cayenne pepper, and black pepper. Bring liquid to a boil. Reduce heat and simmer 1 hour and 10 minutes to

1 hour and 25 minutes or until beans are tender. Remove pot from heat. Remove and discard pork hocks and bay leaves. With a large, shallow spoon, skim fat from top of soup and discard.

Bring soup to a full boil, stirring occasionally. Add pasta to soup. Boil 2 or 3 minutes or until pasta is tender. Add tomato sauce and cook an additional 5 minutes, stirring occasionally, until flavors are blended. Add salt if desired. Since pasta thickens soup after refrigeration, you may want to add a bit more chicken bouillon when reheating.

◆

Number of Servings: 8 *(data per serving)*

calories:	157	protein (gm):	8.8
% calories from fat:	15	fat (gm):	2.6
cholesterol (mg):	11	sodium (mg):	792

WHITE BEAN AND SPINACH SOUP

A delicious, hearty entree with the meaty taste of smoked pork, this soup is a meal in a bowl.

Makes 6 to 8 Servings.

1½ cups dry navy beans
2 teaspoons olive oil
1 large onion, chopped
2 garlic cloves, chopped
6 cups chicken bouillon, reconstituted from cubes or granules, divided
2 cups water
¼ cup pearl barley
1 small pork hock (about 5 ozs.)
2 large carrots, sliced
2 large celery stalks, including leaves, sliced
2 large bay leaves
¾ teaspoon dried marjoram leaves
¾ teaspoon dried basil leaves
½ teaspoon dried thyme leaves
Dash (generous) cayenne pepper
¼ teaspoon black pepper
1 16-oz. can reduced-sodium stewed tomatoes, *or* regular stewed tomatoes
1 10-oz. package chopped frozen spinach, thawed and drained
Salt to taste

Place beans in Dutch oven or small soup pot. Cover them with 2 in. water and bring to a boil over high heat. Lower heat and boil 2 minutes. Remove pot from heat, cover, and let beans stand 1 hour. Drain beans in colander, discarding soaking water.

In the pot in which beans were cooked, combine olive oil, onion, garlic, and 3 tablespoons of bouillon. Cook onion and garlic over medium heat, stirring frequently, 4 to 5 minutes or until onion is soft. If liquid begins to evaporate, add a bit more bouillon. Add remaining bouillon to pot.

Return beans to pot. Add water, barley, pork hock, carrots, celery, bay leaves, marjoram, basil, thyme, cayenne pepper, and black pepper. Bring liquid to a boil. Reduce heat and simmer 1 hour and 10 minutes to 1 hour and 25 minutes or until beans are tender.

Remove pot from heat. Remove and discard pork hock and bay leaves. With a large, shallow spoon, skim fat from top of soup and discard. Add stewed tomatoes and spinach, stirring in and distributing spinach with large spoon. Add salt if desired. Bring soup to a boil, reduce heat, and simmer, stirring occasionally, about 5 to 7 minutes or until spinach is tender.

This soup keeps in refrigerator 3 or 4 days.

Number of Servings: 8 *(data per serving)*

calories:	168	protein (gm):	9.8
% calories from fat:	14	fat (gm):	2.6
cholesterol (mg):	5	sodium (mg):	704

GARBANZO AND COUSCOUS SOUP

Couscous, a quick-cooking, mild-flavored wheat product used in Middle Eastern cuisine, is available in most large grocery stores. In this soup it combines very pleasantly with garbanzo beans.

Makes 6 Servings.

2 teaspoons olive oil
1 medium-sized onion, chopped
1 clove garlic, minced
4 cups chicken bouillon reconstituted from cubes or granules, divided
1 cup water
1 stalk celery, finely chopped
1 large carrot, finely chopped
1 cup zucchini, diced
1 cup small cauliflower pieces
½ medium-sized green pepper, diced
1 16-oz. can tomatoes, including juice
2 cups cooked garbanzo beans, *or* 1 15-oz. can garbanzo beans, rinsed and drained
1 small bay leaf
¾ teaspoon ground cumin
¾ teaspoon dried thyme leaves
1 teaspoon sugar
  Dash ground cloves
  Dash black pepper
⅓ cup couscous
  Salt to taste

In a Dutch oven or small soup pot, combine olive oil, onion, garlic, and 3 tablespoons of bouillon. Cook onion and garlic over medium heat, stirring frequently, until onion is soft, about 5 to 6 minutes. Add remaining bouillon, water, celery, carrot, zucchini, cauliflower, green pepper, tomatoes, garbanzo beans, bay leaf, cumin, thyme, sugar, cloves, and black pepper. Break up tomatoes with large spoon.

Bring mixture to a boil, cover, and reduce heat. Simmer 15 to 20 minutes or until vegetables are tender and flavors are well blended. Bring soup to a full boil, add couscous, and boil 2 minutes. Remove pot from heat and allow soup to stand 5 minutes before serving. Add salt if desired. Remove bay leaf and discard.

This soup keeps in refrigerator 2 to 3 days.

Number of Servings: 6 *(data per serving)*

calories:	215	protein (gm):	10.3
% calories from fat:	15	fat (gm):	3.6
cholesterol (mg):	0	sodium (mg):	722

GARBANZO AND PASTA SOUP

Quick, easy, and good, this soup makes a nice luncheon entree.

Makes 4 to 5 Servings.

2 teaspoons olive oil
1 medium-sized onion, chopped
1 clove garlic, minced
4½ cups chicken broth (defatted)
1 stalk celery, finely chopped
1 large carrot, finely chopped
½ cup zucchini, diced
1 small bay leaf
½ teaspoon dried thyme leaves
½ teaspoon dried basil leaves
Dash black pepper
⅓ cup extra-fine pasta pieces
1 8-oz. can reduced-sodium tomato sauce, *or* regular tomato sauce
2 cups cooked garbanzo beans, *or* 1, 15-oz. can garbanzo beans, rinsed and drained
Salt to taste

I n a Dutch oven or small soup pot, combine olive oil, onion, and garlic. Cook onion and garlic over medium heat, stirring frequently, until onion is soft, about 5 minutes. Add chicken broth, celery, carrot, zucchini, bay leaf, thyme, basil, and pepper. Bring soup to a boil, cover, and reduce heat. Simmer 7 or 8 minutes or until celery is almost tender.

Bring soup to a full boil, add pasta, and cook uncovered until tender, about 4 or 5 minutes. Reduce heat. Add tomato sauce and garbanzo beans. Add salt if desired. Simmer about 5 minutes or until flavors are blended. Remove bay leaf and discard.

Since pasta tends to thicken soup after refrigeration, you may want to add a bit more chicken broth when reheating.

Number of Servings: 5 *(data per serving)*

calories:	243	protein (gm):	14.8
% calories from fat:	16	fat (gm):	4.3
cholesterol (mg):	6	sodium (mg):	421

CHILI LENTIL-CORN SOUP

This lentil-corn soup with a South-of-the-Border flavor makes a filling cold weather supper entree.

Makes 5 to 6 Servings.

    2 teaspoons olive oil
    1 large onion, chopped
    1 clove garlic, chopped
    4 cups beef bouillon, reconstituted from cubes,
      divided
    1 16-oz. can tomatoes, including juice
    ¾ cup dry brown lentils, rinsed and sorted
    1 medium-sized carrot, sliced
    1 stalk celery, sliced
    ¾ cup sweet red pepper, chopped (if unavailable,
      substitute sweet green pepper)
  2½ teaspoons chili powder
    ¾ teaspoon ground cumin
    1 bay leaf
    ⅛ teaspoon black pepper
    1 cup water
  1½ cups frozen corn kernels

In a Dutch oven or medium-sized soup pot, combine olive oil, onion, garlic, and 3 tablespoons of bouillon. Cook onion and garlic over medium heat, stirring frequently, until onion is soft, about 3 to 4 minutes. If liquid begins to evaporate, add more bouillon.

Add tomatoes, breaking them up with spoon. Add remaining bouillon, lentils, carrot, celery, sweet red pepper, chili powder, cumin, bay leaf, black pepper, and water. Bring to a boil. Reduce heat and simmer about 1 hour, stirring occasionally, or until lentils are tender. Remove and discard bay leaf. Add corn. Bring soup to a boil, stirring. Lower heat and simmer an additional 10 minutes.

This soup keeps for 4 to 5 days in refrigerator.

Number of Servings: 6 (data per serving)

calories:	137	protein (gm):	7.0
% calories from fat:	13	fat (gm):	2.0
cholesterol (mg):	0	sodium (mg):	727

LIMA BEAN AND BARLEY SOUP

Makes 5 to 6 Servings.

2   teaspoons canola, safflower, or corn oil
1   large onion, finely chopped
1   large celery stalk, thinly sliced
6   cups water
1   pork hock (about 12 ozs.)
1   16-oz. can tomatoes, including juice
2   chicken bouillon cubes
1   large carrot, thinly sliced
1   cup loose-packed frozen lima beans
½   cup fresh parsley leaves, finely chopped
¼   cup pearl barley
½   cup turnip, peeled and diced
1   small bay leaf
½ to 1 teaspoon sugar, or to taste
¾   teaspoon dried thyme leaves
½   teaspoon dried marjoram leaves
⅛   teaspoon ground celery seed
    Pinch cayenne pepper
⅛   teaspoon black pepper
    Salt to taste

In a Dutch oven or very large saucepan, combine oil with onion and celery. Cook over medium heat, stirring frequently, until onion is tender, about 5 or 6 minutes. Add water, pork hock, and tomatoes, breaking up tomatoes with large spoon. Add all remaining ingredients, except the salt, and stir to blend well. Bring soup to a boil. Cover, lower heat, and simmer soup about 1½ hours or until flavors are well blended and barley has thickened the liquid. Remove and discard ham hock and bay leaf. With a large, shallow spoon, skim fat from top of soup and discard. Add salt if desired.

This soup keeps 3 to 4 days in refrigerator.

Number of Servings: 6 *(data per serving)*

calories:	133	protein (gm):	6.9
% calories from fat:	26	fat (gm):	3.8
cholesterol (mg):	14	sodium (mg):	461

MATZO BALL AND VEGETABLE SOUP

We've added vegetables to the soup stock in this traditional Jewish dish. If you want to try it at home, you'll be glad to know that it isn't really hard to make. What's more, this version cuts more than half of the fat from the matzo balls. We've found that the secret of light, fluffy matzo balls lies in mixing the ingredients very well, chilling thoroughly, handling the uncooked mixture gently when shaping it into balls, and cooking in ample liquid. That is why the directions call for cooking the matzo balls in a large pot of water before transferring them to the soup. Matzo meal is available in the specialty section of many large grocery stores.

Makes 6 Servings.

Matzo Balls

- 1 large egg plus 2 large egg whites
- 1 tablespoon canola, safflower, or corn oil
- ½ cup plus 1 tablespoon matzo meal
- ¼ teaspoon (generous) salt
- 2½ tablespoons chicken stock (pg. 195), *or* broth (defatted)

Soup

- 6 to 8 cups chicken stock (pg. 195), *or* broth (defatted)
- 1 stalk celery, diced
- 1 large carrot, diced
- 1 cup frozen lima beans
- 1½ cups small cauliflower pieces
- ⅛ teaspoon black pepper

T o prepare matzo balls, in a small bowl, lightly beat egg, egg whites, and oil together, using a fork. Add matzo meal, salt, and 2½ tablespoons chicken stock. Stir with medium-sized spoon to combine well, making sure matzo meal is completely moistened. Cover mixture and refrigerate at least 1 hour or up to 6 hours.

When matzo ball mixture is thoroughly chilled, bring 3 quarts of water to a boil in a large pot. To form matzo balls, scoop up about 2 teaspoons of matzo ball mixture and shape into a 1¼-in. ball with moistened fingers. Make sure ball is fairly round and smooth, but do not press it together too tightly. Drop matzo ball into boiling water. Repeat with remaining mixture, making 12 balls. Cover pot, reduce heat, and gently boil matzo balls 30 to 35 minutes.

After matzo balls begin to cook, combine remaining soup stock, celery, carrot, lima beans, cauliflower, and black pepper in Dutch oven or soup pot. Bring it to a boil over medium-high heat. Cover, reduce heat, and cook about 20 to 25 minutes.

When matzo balls are done, remove them from cooking water with slotted spoon and gently place them in chicken stock. Cover and simmer 4 to 5 minutes.

Number of Servings: 6 (data per serving)

calories:	152	protein (gm):	10.7
% calories from fat:	24	fat (gm):	4.0
cholesterol (mg):	36	sodium (mg):	574

DOWN HOME GREEN BEAN SOUP

Green beans, smoked pork hock, and tomatoes combine to give this soup its down-home flavor. Barley and black-eyed peas add extra richness.

Makes 5 to 6 Servings.

2 teaspoons olive oil

1 large onion, chopped

1 large garlic clove, minced

5 cups chicken stock (pg. 195), *or* broth (defatted), divided

2 cups water

1 large carrot, sliced

1 large celery stalk, finely chopped

½ cup dried black-eyed peas, sorted and rinsed

3 tablespoons pearl barley

2 small pork hocks (about ½ lb.)

1 large bay leaf

2½ cups fresh green beans, broken in 2-in. pieces

2 teaspoons dried basil leaves

½ teaspoon dried thyme leaves

¼ teaspoon black pepper

Pinch dried, crushed red (hot) pepper

1 16-oz. can reduced-sodium tomatoes, including juice, *or* regular canned tomatoes

Salt to taste

In a 5- to 6-quart pot, combine olive oil, onion, garlic, and 3 tablespoons of chicken stock. Cook onion and garlic over medium heat, stirring frequently, about 5 or 6 minutes or until onion has softened. If liquid begins to evaporate, add a bit more stock.

Add remaining chicken stock, water, carrot, celery, black-eyed peas, barley, pork hocks, and bay leaf. Bring mixture to a boil. Cover, reduce heat, and simmer about 40 minutes, stirring occasionally, or until black-eyed peas are almost done.

Add green beans, basil, thyme, black pepper, and red pepper. Bring to a full boil, then reduce heat and cook about 35 minutes longer or until green beans have reached desired degree of doneness.

Add tomatoes, breaking them up with spoon. Simmer soup about 5 minutes longer, until flavors are blended. Discard bay leaf and pork hocks. Remove soup from heat and allow it to stand for 5 minutes. Add salt if desired. Then, with large, flat spoon, skim off fat from top and discard.

This soup keeps 3 to 4 days in refrigerator.

Number of Servings: 6 *(data per serving)*

calories:	139	protein (gm):	9.1
% calories from fat:	16	fat (gm):	2.5
cholesterol (mg):	1	sodium (mg):	379

EASY SPINACH-PASTA SOUP WITH BASIL

Makes 4 to 5 Servings.

1 10-oz. package frozen and thawed leaf spinach
2 teaspoons extra-virgin olive oil
1 small onion, finely chopped
1 small garlic clove, minced
6 cups chicken broth (defatted), *or* chicken
   bouillon reconstituted from cubes or granules
1 cup water
¾ cup 2-in.-long pieces of uncooked vermicelli or
   other extra-fine spaghetti
¼ cup fresh basil leaves, chopped, *or*
   1½ tablespoons dried basil leaves
¼ teaspoon black pepper
1 cup Italian style (plum) tomatoes, drained
   and chopped
1 cup cooked garbanzo beans, *or* canned
   garbanzo beans, well drained
2 tablespoons grated Parmesan cheese for
   garnish (optional)

L et spinach drain in colander. Press down to remove as much
excess water as possible. Transfer spinach to cutting board. Trim
away coarse stems and discard. Finely chop spinach and return it to
colander to drain further.

In a very large pot over medium heat, combine oil, onion, and garlic
and cook, stirring frequently, until onion is tender. Add broth and water and
bring mixture to a rolling boil over high heat. Stir in vermicelli and continue
cooking 2 minutes.

Stir spinach, basil, pepper, tomatoes, and beans into pot. Continue
cooking 6 to 7 minutes longer or until spinach and pasta are tender. Serve
immediately, sprinkled with a little grated Parmesan if desired.

Number of Servings: 5 (data per serving)

calories:	210	protein (gm):	14.6
% calories from fat:	19	fat (gm):	4.5
cholesterol (mg):	3	sodium (mg):	607

VEGETARIAN SOUPS

Vegetarian chowders, bisques, and potages have pleasing tastes and textures all their own; yet they can be as robust and satisfying as soups containing meat. In fact, meatless or not, a number of the recipes in this chapter are among our favorites.

Most recipes feature garden-fresh vegetables or hearty beans and grains, which combine to provide high-quality protein. Almost all are relatively quick and easy to prepare—as well as quite inexpensive. Many, like East Indian Lentil Soup, Southwest-Style Potato-Corn Chowder con Queso, Tangy Three-Bean Soup, and Vegetarian Minestrone, are substantial enough to serve as a supper entree.

EAST INDIAN LENTIL SOUP

This hearty but very easy main-dish soup tastes best made with tiny beige Indian lentils available in Indian specialty food stores. However, regular brown lentils can also be used. The cooking time is considerably shorter with some Indian lentils. Because the soup is made with water instead of stock or broth, it does require some salt. For a nice accompaniment, serve with whole-wheat pita bread filled with salad.

Makes 8 to 9 Servings.

2 teaspoons canola, safflower, or corn oil
1 large onion, finely chopped
1 garlic clove, minced
10 cups water, divided
2 cups (1 lb.) dry, small beige Indian lentils, *or* dry regular lentils, picked over and rinsed
2 large celery stalks, including leaves, thinly sliced
1 large carrot, thinly sliced
2 to 3 teaspoons mild curry powder, or to taste
1 teaspoon sugar
¼ teaspoon black pepper
Salt to taste

I n a large soup pot, combine oil, onion, garlic, and 3 tablespoons of water. Cook over medium heat, stirring frequently, until onion is tender, about 5 to 6 minutes. Add all remaining ingredients, except the salt, and bring to a boil. Cover, lower the heat, and simmer 40 minutes to 1½ hours (depending on type of lentils used) or until lentils soften and thicken the soup. Stir occasionally to prevent lentils from sticking to bottom of pot. Add salt if desired.

This soup keeps 3 to 4 days in refrigerator.

Number of Servings: 9 *(data per serving)*

calories:	115	protein (gm):	7.5
% calories from fat:	9	fat (gm):	1.1
cholesterol (mg):	0	sodium (mg):	38

SPICY BARLEY SOUP

◆

A satisfying barley soup enlivened with a flavorful blend of herbs and spices.

◆

Makes 6 to 7 Servings.

1 tablespoon canola, safflower, or corn oil
2 large onions, finely chopped
1 large garlic clove, minced
¼ lb. fresh mushrooms, sliced
   (about 8 medium-sized)
8 cups vegetable stock (see pg. 197), *or*
   4 vegetarian bouillon packets (or cubes)
   reconstituted with 8 cups water, divided
1 large carrot, thinly sliced
2 large celery stalks, thinly sliced
3 tablespoons reduced-sodium tomato paste, *or*
   regular tomato paste
½ cup turnip, peeled and diced
¼ cup pearl barley
¼ cup fresh parsley leaves, chopped
2 large bay leaves
1 teaspoon dried marjoram leaves
½ teaspoon dried thyme leaves
½ teaspoon powdered mustard
¼ teaspoon celery seed
   Dash cayenne pepper
¼ teaspoon black pepper, or to taste

I n a very large saucepan or small soup pot, combine oil, onions, garlic, mushrooms, and 2 tablespoons vegetable stock. Cook over medium heat, stirring frequently, until onion is tender, about 6 or 7 minutes. If liquid begins to evaporate, add a bit more stock.

Add all remaining ingredients, stirring well to thoroughly incorporate tomato paste. Bring mixture to a boil. Cover, lower heat, and simmer about 1½ hours or until barley is tender and has thickened the soup. With a large, shallow spoon, skim oil from surface of soup and discard.

Number of Servings: 7 *(data per serving)*

calories:	105	protein (gm):	4.1
% calories from fat:	20	fat (gm):	2.3
cholesterol (mg):	0	sodium (mg):	483

EASY MEXICAN CORN AND BEAN SOUP

This spicy soup is quick and easy to prepare.

Makes 4 to 5 Servings.

1 tablespoon canola, safflower, or corn oil

1 large onion, finely chopped

1 large garlic clove, minced

2 cups tomato juice

1 medium-sized sweet green pepper, diced

1 16-oz. can reduced-sodium tomatoes, *or* regular canned tomatoes, including juice, pureed in blender or food processor

2 cups cooked kidney beans, *or* 1 16-oz. can kidney beans, drained

2 cups frozen corn kernels

1 tablespoon chili powder

1 teaspoon ground cumin

1 teaspoon sugar

¼ teaspoon black pepper

Salt to taste

I n a very large saucepan or small Dutch oven, combine oil, onion, and garlic. Cook over medium heat, stirring frequently, until onion is limp, about 4 or 5 minutes. If liquid begins to evaporate, add a bit of tomato juice. Add all remaining ingredients, except the salt. Bring soup to a boil. Cover, lower heat, and simmer about 20 to 25 minutes or until flavors are well blended. Skim oil from top of soup and discard. Add salt if desired.

This soup keeps 3 to 4 days in refrigerator.

Number of Servings: 5 *(data per serving)*

calories:	199	protein (gm):	9.1
% calories from fat:	12	fat (gm):	2.6
cholesterol (mg):	0	sodium (mg):	373

TANGY THREE-BEAN SOUP

♦

The spicy barbecue flavor of this dish is a nice change of pace from the usual "tamer" bean soup.

♦

Makes 5 to 6 Servings.

½ cup dry black-eyed peas, picked over and rinsed

½ cup dry baby lima beans, picked over and rinsed

½ cup dry Great Northern beans, picked over and rinsed

6½ cups water

1 large garlic clove, minced

1 large onion, finely chopped

1 large carrot, thinly sliced

1 large celery stalk, thinly sliced

⅛ teaspoon ground cloves

1 large bay leaf

1 15-oz. can tomato sauce

1 to 2 tablespoons packed brown sugar

1 tablespoon apple cider vinegar

1 tablespoon light molasses

½ teaspoon powdered mustard

½ teaspoon chili powder

¼ teaspoon ground celery seed

¼ teaspoon dried thyme leaves

¼ teaspoon paprika

⅛ teaspoon cayenne pepper, or to taste

¼ teaspoon black pepper

Salt to taste

P lace beans (first 3 ingredients) in Dutch oven or small soup pot. Cover them with 2 in. of water. Bring to a boil over high heat and boil 2 minutes. Remove pot from heat and let beans stand, covered, 1 hour. Drain beans in colander and discard soaking liquid.

Return beans to pot in which they were soaked. Add water, garlic, onion, carrot, celery, cloves, and bay leaf. Bring mixture to a boil over high heat. Lower heat, cover pot, and simmer 1¼ to 1½ hours or until beans are very tender and have thickened the soup slightly.

Add all remaining ingredients, except salt, and stir to mix well. Simmer soup an additional 25 to 30 minutes or until flavors are well blended. Add salt if desired. Remove and discard bay leaf.

This soup keeps 3 to 4 days in refrigerator.

Number of Servings: 6 *(data per serving)*

calories:	154	protein (gm):	8.0
% calories from fat:	4	fat (gm):	0.7
cholesterol (mg):	0	sodium (mg):	448

VEGETARIAN MINESTRONE

The combination of vegetables and herbs is particularly appealing in this meatless version of a traditional Italian favorite. If vegetable stock or bouillon are unavailable, a non-vegetarian version can also be made with chicken broth or bouillon.

Makes 5 to 6 Servings.

- 2 teaspoons olive oil
- 1 medium-sized onion, finely chopped
- 1 garlic clove, minced
- 4 cups vegetable stock (pg. 197), *or* 2 vegetable bouillon cubes or packets reconstituted with 4 cups water, divided
- 1 15-oz. can reduced-sodium tomato sauce, *or* regular tomato sauce
- 2 cups cooked garbanzo beans, *or* 1 15-oz. can garbanzo beans, well drained
- 1 large celery stalk, diced
- 1 medium-sized carrot, thinly sliced
- 1 large boiling potato, peeled or unpeeled, cut into ¾-in. cubes
- 1 medium-sized zucchini, diced
- ¼ cup fresh parsley leaves, chopped
- 1 teaspoon dried basil leaves
- ½ teaspoon dried marjoram leaves
- ¼ teaspoon dried thyme leaves
- ⅛ teaspoon ground celery seed
  Dash cayenne pepper
- ¼ teaspoon black pepper
- ½ cup small pasta seashells or macaroni, uncooked
  Salt to taste

In a Dutch oven or very large saucepan, combine olive oil, onion, garlic, and 3 tablespoons of vegetable stock. Cook over medium-high heat, stirring frequently, 5 or 6 minutes, until onion is tender. If liquid begins to evaporate, add a bit more stock.

Add remaining vegetable stock, tomato sauce, garbanzo beans, celery, carrot, potato, and zucchini. Then add parsley, basil, marjoram, thyme, celery seed, cayenne, and pepper. Stir to mix well. Cover and bring to a boil. Lower heat and simmer about 15 minutes.

Bring soup to a boil again. Add pasta. Lower heat again and simmer, stirring occasionally, an additional 15 to 20 minutes or until vegetables and pasta are tender. As pasta thickens the soup, stir to make sure it doesn't stick to bottom of pan.

This soup is best the day it's made since the pasta tends to absorb the liquid. When reheating, add a bit more vegetable stock or bouillon.

Number of Servings: 6 (data per serving)

calories:	248	protein (gm):	11.4
% calories from fat:	14	fat (gm):	3.8
cholesterol (mg):	0	sodium (mg):	309

SOUTHWEST-STYLE POTATO-CORN CHOWDER CON QUESO

Makes 5 Servings.

- 2 teaspoons non-diet, tub-style margarine
- ⅔ cup green onions, chopped, including tops
- 1 tablespoon all-purpose white flour
- 3 cups vegetable stock (pg. 197), *or* vegetable bouillon reconstituted from cubes or granules
- 3½ cups boiling potatoes, peeled and cubed (½-in. cubes)
- 1 large bay leaf
- ½ teaspoon dry mustard
- ¼ teaspoon dried marjoram leaves
- ¼ teaspoon white pepper, or to taste
- 1 10-oz. package frozen yellow corn kernels
- 3 ozs. reduced-fat sharp Cheddar cheese, cut into chunks
- 2½ cups 2% milk
- 1 4-oz. can chopped mild green chilies, well drained
  Finely chopped fresh chives for garnish (optional)

I n a large pot over medium-high heat, melt margarine. Add green onions and cook, stirring, until soft, about 5 minutes. Stir in flour and cook, stirring until smoothly incorporated and lightly browned, about 30 seconds. Gradually add stock, stirring until mixture is smooth and well blended.

Add potatoes, bay leaf, mustard, marjoram, and pepper. Bring mixture to a boil. Lower heat and simmer, covered, 15 minutes; stir frequently to prevent potatoes from sticking to bottom of pot. Add corn and continue simmering about 5 minutes longer, until it is cooked through.

Discard bay leaf. Using a measuring cup, scoop up 1 cup of vegetables and liquid from pot and transfer to blender or food processor. Sprinkle cheese over top. If a blender is used, add ½ cup milk. Blend or process until thoroughly pureed, about 1 minute. Return puree to pot, along with remaining milk and green chilies. Heat, stirring, about 5 minutes longer or until soup just comes to a simmer. Serve immediately, garnished with chopped fresh chives if desired.

Keeps, refrigerated, 2 or 3 days.

Number of Servings: 5 *(data per serving)*

calories:	288	protein (gm):	14.4
% calories from fat:	14	fat (gm):	4.4
cholesterol (mg):	9	sodium (mg):	571

CHILLED SOUPS

For some people, the idea of cold soups takes a bit of getting used to. But a chilled cup or bowl of tangy soup on a hot day can be every bit as appealing as a hot soup on a cold day! Try our West African Curried Chicken Soup, Tangy Zucchini Soup, or Easy Gazpacho and see for yourself.

The techniques for making the recipes that follow are similar to those employed in other chapters. Most of the soups are cooked first and then cooled. This means they're perfect for make-ahead entertaining, as they can be prepared up to a day in advance. On the other hand, because it takes longer than you might imagine to chill hot ingredients, cold soups can't be produced on the spur of the moment. Most taste best well chilled and therefore should be refrigerated at least four or five hours before serving. However, it's possible to speed things up a bit by starting the chilling process in the freezer. Soups placed in the freezer should be checked and stirred often to make sure they don't inadvertently freeze.

Because cooling tends to mute flavors, the best soups to serve chilled are generally those with strong and very distinctive seasonings.

For the same reason, we've also found it necessary to add a bit more salt to cold soups than to those served piping hot.

Note that a number of the soups in this chapter such as West African Curried Chicken Soup, Watercress Soup, and Curried Onion-Potato Soup also taste excellent served hot.

And there are some other soups in this book, such as Celery-Tomato and Creamy Broccoli-Potato, that also taste wonderful cold.

CURRIED ONION-POTATO SOUP

In summer we chill this delicious soup and sip it cold from soup cups. In winter we serve it hot.

Makes 5 to 6 Servings.

2 teaspoons non-diet, tub-style margarine
1 medium-sized garlic clove, minced
3 cups onion, coarsely chopped
1¼ teaspoons ground cumin
1¼ teaspoons ground turmeric
1 teaspoon mild curry powder, or to taste
¼ teaspoon black pepper
 Dash cayenne pepper
4½ cups chicken stock or broth (defatted), divided
2 cups potatoes, peeled and diced
¾ cup whole milk
 Salt to taste
1 to 2 teaspoons finely chopped parsley *or* chives for garnish (optional)

In a large saucepan or small soup pot, melt margarine over medium-low heat. Add garlic, onion, cumin, turmeric, curry powder, black pepper, cayenne pepper, and ¼ cup chicken stock and stir to blend well. Raise heat to medium and cook, stirring frequently, about 8 or 9 minutes until onion is very soft. Add a bit more stock if liquid begins to evaporate.

Add remaining stock and potatoes. Cover and simmer mixture about 15 to 18 minutes or until potatoes are very tender. Remove pot from heat. Let mixture cool slightly.

In batches, blend mixture in blender on low speed for 10 seconds. Then raise speed to high and puree until completely smooth. Rinse out pot and return puree to it. Stir in milk. Cook over low heat an additional 5 minutes. Add salt if desired.

Serve hot or cold. To serve cold, cover and chill soup at least 5 hours or overnight. Stir before serving. Garnish individual servings with sprinkling of parsley or chives if desired.

This soup keeps 2 to 3 days in refrigerator.

Number of Servings: 6 *(data per serving)*

calories:	126	protein (gm):	6.6
% calories from fat:	20	fat (gm):	2.8
cholesterol (mg):	5	sodium (mg):	356

CITRUS-TOMATO SOUP

Makes 4 to 5 Servings.

2 tablespoons onion, finely chopped

1 cup chicken bouillon reconstituted from bouillon cube or granules

2 tablespoons packed light brown sugar

4 cups reduced-sodium tomato juice, *or* regular tomato juice

1/3 cup frozen orange juice concentrate

2 tablespoons lemon juice, preferably fresh

1 to 2 drops Tabasco sauce

Salt to taste

Thin orange half-slices for garnish (optional)

I n a medium-sized saucepan, combine onion and bouillon. Bring to a boil over high heat. Cover, lower heat, and simmer about 6 to 7 minutes until onion is tender.

Meanwhile, combine all remaining ingredients, *except* orange slices, in a glass or ceramic bowl. Add onion-bouillon mixture. Add salt if desired. Cover and refrigerate 4 to 5 hours.

Serve soup in cups or small bowls. If desired, cut 1/2-in. slit in diameter of each orange slice so that it can be positioned over side of cup.

This soup keeps 2 to 3 days in refrigerator.

Number of Servings: 5 *(data per serving)*

calories:	106	protein (gm):	2.4
% calories from fat:	2	fat (gm):	0.2
cholesterol (mg):	0	sodium (mg):	196

West African Curried Chicken Soup

Pineapple and curry team up to give this soup its pleasing flavor. We like to serve it as a first course to a summer dinner or luncheon. If you like, it can also be served hot. The recipe calls for a cooked chicken breast half. This can be poached in a small amount of broth or cooked in a microwave.

Makes 4 to 5 servings.

2 teaspoons non-diet, tub-style margarine
2 celery stalks, diced
1 small onion, finely chopped
1 medium-sized garlic clove, minced
3½ cups chicken broth (defatted), divided
1½ to 2 teaspoons mild curry powder, or to taste
3½ tablespoons all-purpose white flour
1 8-oz. can crushed pineapple, well drained
1 small chicken breast half, cooked, boned, and skinned and cut into ½-in. pieces
¾ cup whole milk

I n a Dutch oven or large saucepan, melt margarine over medium heat. Add celery, onion, garlic, and about 3 tablespoons of chicken broth. Cook, stirring frequently, about 5 minutes or until onion is soft. Remove pan from heat. In a small bowl, blend together curry powder and flour. Add this mixture to pan and stir with wooden spoon to blend well.

Return pan to heat. Cook over medium heat, stirring, for 1 minute. Gradually add 1 cup more chicken broth, stirring constantly with wire whisk or wooden spoon until mixture is smooth. Add remaining chicken broth. Bring mixture to a boil. Then cover, lower heat, and simmer about 20 minutes.

Remove pan from heat. Add pineapple, chicken, and milk and stir to mix well. Cover and chill soup at least 5 hours or overnight.

This soup keeps 2 to 3 days in refrigerator.

Number of Servings: 5 *(data per serving)*

calories:	149	protein (gm):	14.1
% calories from fat:	25	fat (gm):	4.1
cholesterol (mg):	28	sodium (mg):	372

EASY GAZPACHO

If the yen for gazpacho—a big favorite in Spain—strikes, and fresh tomatoes are unavailable, try this version, which requires no cooking. The secret of success lies in using good quality canned tomatoes and pureeing them along with the garlic before the other vegetables are added. If you like gazpacho with a very fine texture, you can use a processor to chop the vegetables.

Makes 4 to 6 Servings.

2	14½ oz. cans Italian plum tomatoes
1	small garlic clove, minced
1 to 2	tablespoons chopped scallions *or* chives, or to taste
1	medium-sized cucumber, peeled, seeded, and diced
1	celery stalk, diced
½	large sweet green pepper, diced
2 to 3	drops Tabasco sauce, or to taste
¼	teaspoon black pepper
	Salt to taste
4 to 6	fresh parsley sprigs for garnish (optional)

In a food processor or blender, puree tomatoes and garlic. Transfer mixture to medium-sized glass or ceramic bowl. Add remaining ingredients and stir to mix well. Cover and refrigerate at least 4 hours or overnight. Stir well before serving. If desired, garnish each serving with fresh parsley sprig.

This soup keeps 2 to 3 days in refrigerator.

Number of Servings: 6 *(data per serving)*

calories:	37	protein (gm):	1.7
% calories from fat:	10	fat (gm):	0.4
cholesterol (mg):	0	sodium (mg):	230

SHRIMP GAZPACHO

This soup requires no cooking, yet the pleasing combination of shrimp, vegetables, and spices makes it an excellent hot-weather appetizer. To reduce fat, omit the olive oil. If you like gazpacho with a fine texture, you can use a food processor to chop the vegetables.

Makes 5 to 6 Servings.

2 cups tomato juice
2 teaspoons olive oil
¾ teaspoon prepared horseradish
½ teaspoon chili powder
¼ teaspoon (generous) salt
⅛ teaspoon dried thyme leaves
   Pinch (generous) cayenne pepper
2 medium-large, vine-ripened tomatoes, cored and finely chopped
1 medium-sized cucumber, peeled, seeded, and finely chopped
½ medium sweet green pepper, finely chopped
2 tablespoons scallions *or* chives, chopped
1 small clove garlic, minced
1 cup medium-sized cooked shrimp
1 tablespoon finely chopped fresh parsley leaves *or* chives for garnish (optional)

In a medium-sized, non-corrosive bowl, stir together tomato juice and olive oil. Stir in horseradish, chili powder, salt, thyme, and cayenne pepper. Stir to mix well. Add tomatoes, cucumber, green pepper, scallions, and garlic and stir well. Stir in shrimp. Refrigerate the gazpacho, covered, at least 3½ hours and up to 12 hours before serving.

Serve in bowls or mugs. Garnish individual servings with light sprinkling of parsley or chives if desired.

This soup keeps 2 or 3 days in refrigerator.

Number of Servings: 6 *(data per serving)*

calories:	65	protein (gm):	5.8
% calories from fat:	28	fat (gm):	2.0
cholesterol (mg):	41	sodium (mg):	442

TANGY ZUCCHINI SOUP

◆

*Buttermilk is a subtle addition to this unusual cold soup.
For an even tangier and lower-fat version, use more buttermilk
and less whole milk.*

Makes 4 to 5 Servings.

1 medium-sized onion, finely chopped
1 small garlic clove, minced
2 cups zucchini, diced
½ cup potato, peeled and diced
3 cups chicken bouillon reconstituted from
   cubes or granules
2 tablespoons fresh parsley leaves, chopped
¼ teaspoon powdered mustard
⅛ teaspoon white pepper
   Dash (generous) cayenne pepper
½ cup commercial buttermilk*
½ cup whole milk*
   Salt to taste
   Zucchini slices, thin, for garnish, (optional)

In a medium-sized saucepan, combine onion, garlic, zucchini, potato, bouillon, parsley, mustard, white pepper, and cayenne. Bring to a boil over high heat. Cover, lower heat, and simmer 12 to 15 minutes until potato is very tender. Remove pan from heat. Cool mixture slightly.

In batches, blend in blender on low speed for 10 seconds. Then raise speed to high and puree until almost completely smooth but some parsley flecks remain. Transfer puree to medium-sized glass or ceramic bowl. Stir in buttermilk and milk.

Cover and chill 4 to 5 hours. Taste soup; add salt if desired. Serve in cups or small bowls. If desired, garnish each serving with thin zucchini slice.

This soup keeps 2 to 3 days in refrigerator.

Number of Servings: 5 *(data per serving)*

calories:	63	protein (gm):	3.3
% calories from fat:	17	fat (gm):	1.2
cholesterol (mg):	4	sodium (mg):	560

*Note: To reduce fat in this recipe, increase amount of buttermilk and decrease whole milk. *Or* use 2% milk.

CHILLED CAULIFLOWER SOUP

This soup is a nice way to start a summer lunch and is also good as a refreshing afternoon snack. Low-fat milk works very well in this recipe, but you may substitute whole milk for extra richness.

Makes 4 to 6 Servings.

1 small onion, finely chopped
1 small clove garlic, chopped
1¾ cups chicken broth or stock (defatted), divided
¾ cup potato, peeled and diced
2 cups small cauliflower pieces, including stems
⅛ teaspoon white pepper
⅛ teaspoon (generous) dill weed
¾ cup 2% milk*
¼ teaspoon lemon juice, preferably fresh
Chopped chives for garnish

I n a medium-sized pot, combine onion, garlic, and 3 tablespoons stock. Cook over medium heat, stirring occasionally, 4 or 5 minutes or until onion is soft. If liquid begins to evaporate, add a bit more stock. Add remainder of stock, potatoes, cauliflower, white pepper, and dill weed.

Bring to a boil over high heat. Lower heat, cover, and simmer about 11 to 14 minutes until potatoes and cauliflower are tender. Remove pot from heat.

In batches if necessary, puree mixture in blender. Return puree to pot in which it was cooked. Add milk and lemon juice, and stir to mix well. Simmer an additional 4 or 5 minutes.

Transfer soup to medium-sized bowl. Cover and chill at least 5 hours or overnight. Stir before serving. Serve in small bowls or soup cups. Garnish individual servings with sprinkling of chopped chives if desired.

This soup keeps in refrigerator 2 to 3 days.

Number of Servings: 6   *(data per serving)*

calories:	56	protein (gm):	3.7
% calories from fat:	13	fat (gm):	0.8
cholesterol (mg):	2	sodium (mg):	146

*Note: To reduce fat in this soup, substitute 1% milk.

WATERCRESS SOUP

Here's a soup that celebrates the pungent, peppery taste of fresh watercress. The watercress itself is not cooked, which preserves the characteristic flavor of the fresh herb. If desired, the soup can also be served hot.

Makes 4 to 5 Servings.

1 lb. leeks (about 3 medium)
1 tablespoon non-diet, tub-style margarine
1 medium-sized onion, chopped
3 cups chicken bouillon, reconstituted from cubes, divided
1¾ cups potatoes, peeled and diced
1 teaspoon lemon juice, preferably fresh
⅛ teaspoon white pepper
1 cup watercress leaves and tender stems, coarsely chopped
1 cup whole milk

Trim off and discard root ends of leeks and all but about 1 in. of green tops. Peel off and discard one or two layers of the tough outer leaves. Then, beginning at green end, slice down about 1 in. into leeks. Put leeks into colander. Wash them thoroughly under cool running water, separating layers to remove grit trapped between them. Wash again to remove all traces of grit. Then set leeks aside until well-drained. Cut leeks into ½-in. pieces.

In a medium-sized saucepan, melt margarine over medium heat. Add leeks, onion, and 3 tablespoons of bouillon and cook, stirring frequently, about 5 or 6 minutes or until leeks are tender. If the liquid begins to evaporate, add a bit more bouillon. Add potatoes and remaining bouillon. Bring mixture to a boil over medium-high heat. Cover, lower heat, and simmer about 12 to 14 minutes or until potatoes and leeks are very tender. Cool mixture slightly. Add lemon juice and pepper and stir well.

In batches, blend mixture in blender on low speed for 10 seconds. Then raise speed to high and puree until completely smooth. Stir in watercress and blend on low, with on/off pulses, just enough to break up leaves and stems. Transfer soup to medium-sized bowl. Stir in milk. Cover and chill at least 5 hours. Serve in small bowls or cups.

Alternatively, to serve the soup hot, after blending, return mixture to pot in which it was cooked. Stir in milk and cook over medium heat just until heated through. Serve.

This soup keeps 2 to 3 days in refrigerator.

Number of Servings: 5 *(data per serving)*

calories:	174	protein (gm):	4.9
% calories from fat:	23	fat (gm):	4.4
cholesterol (mg):	7	sodium (mg):	598

SUMMERTIME CELERY SOUP

Makes 5 to 6 Servings.

⅔ cup boiling water

1¼ teaspoons fennel seeds

1 teaspoon olive oil, preferably extra-virgin

3 cups celery (7 or 8 medium stalks), coarsely chopped

8 medium-sized green onions, including tops, coarsely chopped

1 small garlic clove, minced

4 cups chicken bouillon reconstituted from bouillon cubes or granules, divided

2½ tablespoons uncooked long-grain white rice

3 tablespoons fresh chives, finely chopped *or* 1½ tablespoons dried chives

⅛ teaspoon white pepper

Finely chopped chives for garnish (optional)

Small dollops of non-fat plain yogurt for garnish (optional)

Pour boiling water over fennel seeds in a cup. Set aside to steep while other ingredients are prepared.

In 3- to 4-quart saucepan over medium heat, combine olive oil, celery, onions, and garlic. Cook, stirring, until onion is slightly soft, about 4 minutes. Add 2½ cups bouillon, rice, chives, and white pepper to pan. Bring mixture to a boil. Lower heat and simmer, covered, about 20 minutes or until celery and rice are tender. Set mixture aside to cool slightly.

In batches, blend mixture in blender on low speed for 10 seconds. Raise speed to high and continue blending until mixture is completely pureed and smooth. Transfer the batches of puree to a storage container. Stir in remaining bouillon.

Strain the water in which the fennel seed is soaking through a fine sieve directly into soup; discard fennel seeds. Cover and refrigerate soup at least 3 hours and up to 8 hours before serving. Thin soup with a little water before serving, if too thick.

Serve soup in small bowls, garnished with chopped fresh chives and small dollops of yogurt if desired.

Number of Servings: 6 *(data per serving)*

calories:	45	protein (gm):	1.8
% calories from fat:	20	fat (gm):	1.0
cholesterol (mg):	0	sodium (mg):	635

ZESTY TOMATO-VEGETABLE SOUP

Makes 5 to 6 Servings.

1½ teaspoons olive oil, preferably extra-virgin
1 medium-sized onion, coarsely chopped
1 large celery stalk, coarsely chopped
1 medium-sized carrot, coarsely chopped
¾ cup sweet red pepper, chopped
1 cup beef stock (pg. 199), *or* beef broth (defatted)
1 35-oz. can imported Italian (plum) tomatoes, including juice
¼ cup dry red wine
1 teaspoon lemon juice
¾ teaspoon celery salt
Pinch (generous) dried, crushed red (hot) pepper, or to taste
Finely chopped fresh chives for garnish

I n a 3- to 4-quart pot over medium heat, combine olive oil, onion, and celery. Cook, stirring, until onion is slightly soft, about 4 minutes. Add carrot and sweet red pepper and continue cooking 3 to 4 minutes longer, stirring, until vegetables are limp and most liquid has evaporated from pot.

Stir in all remaining ingredients, except chives, and bring mixture to a boil over medium-high heat. Lower heat and simmer, covered, 10 minutes. Remove pot from heat and let mixture cool slightly.

Working in batches, transfer mixture to blender. Blend on low speed 10 seconds; then raise speed to high and blend until completely pureed and smooth. Transfer soup to noncorrosive storage container, and chill at least 4 hours and up to 48 hours before serving.

Ladle soup into small bowls or soup cups. Garnish servings with chopped chives.

Number of Servings: 6 *(data per serving)*

calories:	68	protein (gm):	2.5
% calories from fat:	23	fat (gm):	1.7
cholesterol (mg):	0	sodium (mg):	616

DILLY ICED CARROT SOUP

This is very refreshing on a sultry day.

Makes 5 to 6 Servings.

2 teaspoons non-diet, tub-style margarine

1 cup onion, coarsely chopped

1 tablespoon all-purpose flour

3⅓ cups chicken stock (see pg. 195), *or* broth (defatted), divided

2½ cups carrots (about 1 lb.), chopped

¾ cup potato, peeled and diced

¼ teaspoon salt, or to taste

⅛ teaspoon white pepper

⅓ cup low-fat plain yogurt

1 tablespoon fresh dill weed, coarse stems removed, *or* 1 teaspoon dried dill weed

Dill weed sprigs for garnish (optional)

In a 3-quart saucepan over medium heat, melt margarine. Add onion and cook, stirring, until slightly soft, about 4 minutes. Stir in flour until well blended and continue cooking 30 seconds longer, stirring. Gradually add 2 cups of stock, stirring until smoothly incorporated into flour mixture. Add carrots, potato, salt, and white pepper and bring mixture to a boil over medium-high heat.

Lower heat and simmer, covered and stirring occasionally, 12 to 15 minutes or until carrots are just cooked through. Remove pan from heat and let mixture cool slightly.

Transfer mixture to blender. Blend on low speed 10 seconds; then raise speed to high and blend until completely pureed and smooth. Transfer soup to noncorrosive storage container.

Combine remaining 1⅓ cups stock and yogurt in blender. Blend a few seconds until thoroughly combined. Stir yogurt mixture and dill weed into soup storage container. Refrigerate at least 4 hours and up to 48 hours before serving.

Ladle soup into small bowls or soup cups. Garnish servings with sprig of dill weed if desired.

Number of Servings: 6 *(data per serving)*

calories:	103	protein (gm):	5.1
% calories from fat:	17	fat (gm):	1.9
cholesterol (mg):	1	sodium (mg):	380

FRUIT SOUPS

SPICY APPLE-WINE SOUP

This sweet, spicy soup is an interesting way to serve apples, and it works well as a luncheon first course or as a dessert.

Makes 4 to 5 Servings.

6 ¼-whole cloves
2 ¼-in.-thick lemon slices, seeds removed
½ cup Burgundy wine
2 cups white grape juice, divided
2 cups tart apples, peeled and coarsely chopped
1 3-in.-long cinnamon stick

171

2 tablespoons mild honey
1 tablespoon sugar
1½ tablespoons cornstarch
⅛ cup golden raisins
4 to 5 tablespoons non-fat vanilla yogurt, *or*
reduced-fat sour cream (for garnish)

S tick cloves into lemon slices. In a small saucepan, combine wine, 1¾ cups grape juice, apples, cinnamon stick, honey, sugar, and clove-studded lemon slices. Bring mixture to a boil over medium-high heat. Lower heat, cover, and simmer about 11 to 13 minutes or until apples are tender when pierced with fork.

Meanwhile, stir together cornstarch and remaining ¼ cup grape juice. When apples are tender, remove cinnamon stick, lemon slices, and clove. Then add cornstarch-grape juice mixture to apples and cook, stirring, until liquid in pan thickens, about 1 or 2 minutes. Add raisins and simmer an additional 2 minutes.

To serve, ladle soup into cups or small bowls. Top each serving with tablespoon of non-fat yogurt or light sour cream.

This soup keeps 2 or 3 days in refrigerator.

◆

Number of Servings: 5 *(data per serving)*

calories:	166	protein (gm):	1.5
% calories from fat:	2	fat (gm):	0.3
cholesterol (mg):	0	sodium (mg):	28

CANTALOUPE-LIME COOLER

A tangy refresher on a hot day, this soup is high in vitamin C. Serve icy cold as an appetizer, a snack, or a light dessert. You may like the soup with a bit of texture. Or it can be pureed until completely smooth.

Makes 4 to 5 Servings.

¼ cup sugar
1 tablespoon cornstarch
   Dash (generous) salt
¾ cup cold water
½ large cantaloupe, peeled, seeded, and cut into
   1-in. chunks (about 4 cups)
   Zest, grated, from 1 lime (green part of peel)
1 tablespoon (generous) fresh lime juice
   Thin lime slices for garnish (optional)

S tir together sugar, cornstarch, and salt in small saucepan. Gradually stir in water until mixture is smooth. Bring to a boil over medium heat and cook, stirring about 1 minute or until mixture thickens. Set aside to cool slightly.

In a blender, combine sugar-water mixture with cantaloupe. Blend on low speed until all pieces are partially pureed. Then raise speed to high, and blend until desired consistency is reached. Transfer to medium-sized bowl. Stir in lime zest and lime juice. Cover and chill 4 to 5 hours or overnight. Stir before serving. If desired, garnish individual portions with small slice of lime.

This soup keeps 1 or 2 days in refrigerator.

Number of Servings: 5 *(data per serving)*

calories:	88	protein (gm):	1.1
% calories from fat:	4	fat (gm):	0.4
cholesterol (mg):	0	sodium (mg):	11

STRAWBERRY-PEAR SOUP

Pears are a subtle yet pleasing addition to this chilled soup. The recipe also utilizes the liquid from juice-packed canned pears. If there isn't quite enough juice in the can to make one cup, add a little bit of water.

Makes 4 to 5 Servings.

4 cups strawberries, hulled and coarsely sliced
½ cup water
1 cup juice from juice-packed canned pear halves
4 juice-packed canned pear halves
2 teaspoons lemon juice, preferably fresh
¼ cup sugar, or more to taste
Strawberry slices for garnish (optional)

In 2 batches, combine strawberries and water in blender container. Blend until strawberries are completely pureed. Press mixture through a fine sieve. Discard strawberry seeds.

In batches, if necessary, return puree to blender container. Add all remaining ingredients, except the strawberry slices for garnish, and blend until soup is completely smooth. Transfer soup to a glass or ceramic bowl. Cover and chill 3 to 4 hours before serving. Garnish with strawberry slices if desired.

This soup keeps 2 to 3 days in refrigerator.

Number of Servings: 5 *(data per serving)*

calories:	120	protein (gm):	0.9
% calories from fat:	4	fat (gm):	0.5
cholesterol (mg):	0	sodium (mg):	5

WATERMELON GAZPACHO

Instead of using pureed or chopped tomatoes as a foundation and adding zesty vegetables to make a soup, in this fanciful creation we use watermelon and a colorful array of fruits to the same end. The result is a light and beautiful fruit soup that can be served as a first course, a side dish, or a simple, refreshing dessert.

Makes 4 to 5 Servings.

- 5 lbs. fresh watermelon (about ¼ of a medium-large watermelon)
- ¼ teaspoon (generous) peeled and very finely minced fresh ginger root
- 2 tablespoons sugar, or a little more to taste
- 1½ tablespoons fresh lemon juice
- ½ cup ripe mango, *or* fresh peach, peeled and finely diced
- ½ cup dark sweet cherries, pitted and diced
- ⅓ cup green seedless grapes, quartered
- ⅓ cup fresh blueberries
- ⅛ teaspoon lemon zest, very finely grated

  Mint sprigs or chopped fresh mint leaves for garnish (optional)

S eed and cut enough chunks from watermelon to make 2¾ cups. Combine seeded chunks, ginger root, sugar, and lemon juice in blender or processor. Blend or process until completely smooth. Transfer puree to a large, noncorrosive bowl.

Seed and dice remainder of flavorful watermelon flesh; discard rind and lighter-colored flesh. Add diced watermelon, mango, cherries, grapes, blueberries, and lemon zest to puree. Cover and refrigerate 3 to 4 hours or until well chilled; do not keep longer than 12 hours.

Serve immediately in pre-chilled small glass bowls or soup cups. Garnish servings with mint if desired.

Number of Servings: 5 *(data per serving)*

calories:	169	protein (gm):	2.6
% calories from fat:	10	fat (gm):	1.8
cholesterol (mg):	0	sodium (mg):	8

ICED STRAWBERRY-BUTTERMILK SOUP

Pretty as well as zesty and refreshing, this soup is a great addition to a warm-weather brunch or luncheon menu. The rhubarb and buttermilk add zing without being identifiable on their own.

Makes 4 to 5 Servings.

- 3 cups loose-packed frozen cut rhubarb, partially thawed
- ¾ cup granulated sugar (or more, to taste)
- ½ cup cranberry juice cocktail, divided
- 1 tablespoon fresh lemon juice
- 1½ tablespoons cornstarch
- 3 tablespoons Grand Marnier, *or* kirsch (cherry liqueur), *or* orange juice
- 2⅔ cups ripe strawberries, hulled, *or* frozen (partially thawed) loose-packed whole strawberries
- 1½ cups buttermilk (approximately), divided
- 1 teaspoon vanilla extract

Fresh or frozen strawberry slices for garnish

$\boxed{\text{I}}$ n a medium-sized saucepan, stir together rhubarb, sugar, and ¼ cup cranberry juice over medium heat. Bring mixture to a simmer, stirring. Simmer, stirring occasionally, 7 to 9 minutes or until rhubarb is very tender.

Meanwhile, stir together remaining ¼ cup cranberry juice, lemon juice, cornstarch, and Grand Marnier in a cup until well blended and smooth. Stir cornstarch mixture into rhubarb mixture until smoothly incorporated. Cook, stirring, about 2 minutes longer or until mixture thickens and becomes clear.

In batches, transfer mixture to blender. Blend until completely pureed and smooth, about 2 minutes for each batch. If mixture looks and tastes smooth at this point, transfer it to storage container. If bits of rhubarb remain, strain mixture through a fine sieve into storage container.

Combine strawberries, 1¼ cups buttermilk, and vanilla in blender. Blend until very smooth. Strain the puree through a very fine sieve into a bowl, pressing down on the solids with a large spoon to force through as much juice and pulp as possible: discard seeds. Stir strained strawberries into rhubarb mixture. Add sugar to taste if soup is too tart; stir until sugar dissolves. Place soup in freezer for 1½ to 2½ hours or until very cold and a few ice crystals have formed around edges but mixture is not frozen.

Stir soup to break up any ice crystals. Divide soup among small, chilled bowls. Pour about 2 teaspoons of buttermilk into center of each bowl. Using small spoon, stir once through soup and buttermilk to produce a swirled effect. Garnish each serving with several strawberry slices and serve immediately.

Keeps up to 24 hours in refrigerator.

Number of Servings: 5 *(data per serving)*

calories:	376	protein (gm):	3.5
% calories from fat:	2	fat (gm):	1.0
cholesterol (mg):	3	sodium (mg):	81

BLUEBERRY SOUP

A light and pretty soup, featuring whole blueberries in a blueberry-wine sauce. This is great served as a brunch or luncheon first course, or as a refreshing dessert.

Makes 5 Servings.

    4 cups fresh or loose-packed frozen and thawed
       blueberries, divided
    ¼ cup fresh lemon juice
 ½ to ⅔ cup granulated sugar, depending on
       sweetness of berries
    2 tablespoons cornstarch
    ⅛ teaspoon ground cinnamon
    1 cup cranberry juice cocktail
    1 cup dry white wine
    1 ½-in.-thick lemon slice, seeds removed
    1 teaspoon vanilla extract, divided
    ¾ cup low-fat vanilla yogurt

In a medium-sized saucepan, stir together half the berries and lemon juice. Bring mixture to a simmer over medium-high heat. Cook, stirring, about 2 minutes or until berries begin to exude juices. Transfer berry mixture to blender or food processor. Blend or process until mixture is pureed.

Thoroughly stir together ½ cup sugar, cornstarch, and cinnamon in saucepan previously used. Stir in cranberry juice until mixture is well blended and smooth. Turn out blueberry puree into a very fine sieve set over the saucepan. Using back of large spoon, press blueberry pulp and juice through sieve, discarding skins and seeds. Add wine and lemon slice to pan.

Bring mixture to a boil, stirring, over medium-high heat. Lower heat and simmer, stirring about 2 minutes longer, until mixture thickens slightly and becomes clear. Remove pan from heat and stir in half the vanilla. Stir in a little more sugar to taste if mixture is too tart.

Refrigerate berry mixture until cooled. Discard lemon slice. Stir in remaining 2 cups blueberries. Chill soup, covered, at least 3½ hours and up to 24 hours before serving.

To serve, stir together yogurt and remaining vanilla. Divide soup among soup cups or small bowls. Add a generous dollop of yogurt to center of each serving.

Number of Servings: 5 *(data per serving)*

calories:	219	protein (gm):	0.8
% calories from fat:	4	fat (gm):	0.9
cholesterol (mg):	0	sodium (mg):	35

ICED RED PLUM SOUP WITH BRANDY

◆

This tangy fruit soup takes advantage of the abundance of good summer plums. For best results, choose tart, flavorful, red-skinned plums.

◆

Makes 5 to 6 Servings.

1¾ lbs. fully-ripe, tart red plums (about 14 medium-sized), halved and pitted
1 cup granulated sugar (or more, to taste)
½ cup cranberry juice cocktail
1½ cups low-fat vanilla yogurt
2 tablespoons kirsch (cherry liqueur)
1 teaspoon vanilla extract
Sugar to taste
Very thin slices of fresh plum for garnish

I n a medium-sized saucepan, stir together plums, cup sugar, and cranberry juice. Bring mixture to a boil over medium-high heat. Lower heat and simmer, covered, 6 to 10 minutes or until plums are soft. In 2 batches, transfer plums to blender. Blend until plum flesh and skins are completely pureed and smooth, about 2 minutes for each batch.

Transfer puree to noncorrosive storage container and stir in yogurt, liqueur, and vanilla until evenly incorporated. Add sugar to taste if soup is too tart; stir until sugar dissolves. If mixture is thick, add a tablespoon or two of water to thin soup consistency.

Place the soup in freezer 2 to 3 hours, until it is very cold and just slightly frozen at edges. (If mixture freezes further, whisk it with wire whisk until it thaws again before serving.)

Divide soup among small bowls, preferably chilled. Arrange several plum slices, pinwheel fashion, in center of each serving.

Keeps, refrigerated, 2 days.

◆

Number of Servings: 6 *(data per serving)*

calories:	280	protein (gm):	3.5
% calories from fat:	5	fat (gm):	1.4
cholesterol (mg):	2	sodium (mg):	34

CROCK POT SOUPS

I f the idea of coming home to a piping hot meal after a hard day at work sounds appealing, thumb through the recipes in this chapter. They're all intended for slow, no-fuss crock pot cookery.

There's a wide selection to choose from, including Easy Goulash Soup, Workday Bean Soup, Sweet and Sour Ground Round and Vegetable Soup, and Chicken and Barley Soup. All are filling entrees.

If you've used a crock pot before, you know there are certain techniques that help ensure success. If you're new to this type of cookery, be sure to read the directions that come with the appliance before proceeding.

In general, soups cooked in the crock pot need less water than conventionally prepared recipes. That's because the low cooking temperature makes for little or no evaporation. Also, meat tends to cook more quickly than vegetables, so carrots, celery, potatoes, and onions need to be diced or cut into small pieces. (When you plan to start cooking a crock-pot soup in the morning but know you're going to be in a hurry, you may want to dice the vegetables the night before and refrigerate them.) When filling the crock pot, remember that vegetables cook best at the bottom of the pot where they get more heat.

We've also found that crock pot cookery changes the tastes of some foods. A number of seasonings such as bay are intensified—so you may want to use less than in a conventional recipe. Others such as onion and chili powder actually become more mellow—so you may need more than usual. Also, soups have more flavor if they include broth or bouillon.

In general, we've discovered that it isn't necessary to brown meat before putting it into the crock pot. The one exception is ground beef, which looks more attractive if browned first, using conventional methods.

Most crock pots have only 2 temperature settings—high and low. But within these settings, we've found considerable variation in the cooking times for pots produced by different manufacturers. That's one reason the cooking directions are fairly flexible in the recipes that follow.

Another point to remember is that lifting the lid during cooking will significantly lengthen the time needed. Therefore, it's a good idea to leave the pot undisturbed except when additional ingredients are added.

We recommend starting soups on high to raise meat to a safe temperature more quickly. If you don't have time to cook the soup on high for an hour, you can bring the ingredients to a boil in a conventional pot on the stove and then transfer them to the crock pot, with setting on low. Also, it rarely hurts to cook a crock pot soup an hour or two after the ingredients are tender, if that turns out to be most convenient.

With the majority of crock pots, 2 hours of cooking on low equal 1 hour of cooking on high. So, although the recipes in this chapter call for most of the cooking at the low setting, you can usually halve the cooking time by simply shifting to the high setting.

LENTIL SOUP

Makes 5 to 7 Servings.

1 lb. dry brown lentils (2⅓ cups) picked over
   and rinsed
1 large onion, finely chopped
1 large celery stalk, grated or shredded
1 large carrot, grated or shredded
8 cups very hot tap water
1 large pork hock (about 1 lb.)
2 teaspoons sugar
¼ teaspoon powdered mustard
   Dash cayenne pepper
2 beef bouillon cubes
½ teaspoon dried thyme leaves
¼ teaspoon black pepper

Combine all ingredients in crock pot and stir to mix seasonings.
Cover and cook on high setting 10 to 12 hours or until lentils are
very tender and soup has thickened. Remove pork hock and discard. With
large, shallow spoon, skim fat from surface of soup and discard. Stir soup
before serving.

This soup keeps 4 to 5 days in refrigerator.

Number of Servings: 7 *(data per serving)*

calories:	190	protein (gm):	14.4
% calories from fat:	10	fat (gm):	2.1
cholesterol (mg):	2	sodium (mg):	313

SWEET-AND-SOUR GROUND ROUND AND VEGETABLE SOUP

◆

Because ground beef should be browned by conventional methods before being cooked in the crock pot, this soup is started on the stove and then transferred to the slow cooker.

◆

Makes 5 to 6 Servings.

¾ lb. ground beef round
1 large onion, finely chopped
2 large garlic cloves, minced
1 15-oz. can reduced-sodium tomato sauce, *or* regular tomato sauce
2 large celery stalks, diced
1 medium-sized potato, peeled or unpeeled, diced
1 large carrot, thinly sliced
2 tablespoons pearl barley, uncooked
5 cups very hot tap water
2 beef bouillon cubes
1 cup frozen corn kernels
1 cup loose-packed frozen baby lima beans
2 tablespoons packed light brown sugar
2 tablespoons apple cider vinegar
¾ teaspoon powdered mustard
¾ teaspoon dried thyme leaves
1 large bay leaf
¼ teaspoon black pepper
Salt to taste

I n a Dutch oven, combine ground round, onion, and garlic. Cook over medium heat, stirring frequently and breaking up the meat with spoon, until meat is browned. With slotted spoon, transfer mixture to a plate lined with paper towels. When fat has been absorbed by paper towels, return meat to Dutch oven.

Add all remaining ingredients, except the salt, and bring to a boil. Then transfer mixture to crock pot. Cover and cook at low heat 7 to 9 hours or until barley has thickened the soup and vegetables are tender. Skim fat from top of soup with large, shallow spoon and discard along with bay leaf. Stir soup before serving. Add salt if desired.

This soup keeps 4 to 5 days in refrigerator.

◆

Number of Servings: 6 *(data per serving)*

calories:	249	protein (gm):	15.3
% calories from fat:	24	fat (gm):	6.7
cholesterol (mg):	33	sodium (mg):	372

CHICKEN AND BARLEY SOUP

Makes 6 to 7 Servings.

2 large chicken breast halves, skin and bones removed
4½ cups chicken stock (pg. 195), *or* broth (defatted)
1 cup water
⅓ cup pearl barley
1 large onion, finely chopped
1 garlic clove, minced
1 large carrot, grated or shredded
1 large celery stalk, grated or shredded
¼ cup fresh parsley leaves, chopped
½ teaspoon dried thyme leaves
⅛ teaspoon ground celery seed
1 large bay leaf
¼ teaspoon black pepper
Salt to taste

Combine all ingredients, except salt, in crock pot. Cover and cook on high 1 hour. Change setting to low and cook an additional 7 to 8 hours or until barley is tender and has thickened soup slightly.

Remove chicken and reserve it in medium-sized bowl. With a large, shallow spoon, skim off and discard fat from top of soup. When chicken is cool enough to handle, cut meat into bite-sized pieces. Return meat to soup and cook an additional 10 minutes. Add salt if desired. Stir soup before serving.

This soup keeps 3 to 4 days in refrigerator.

Number of Servings: 7 *(data per serving)*

calories:	148	protein (gm):	19.8
% calories from fat:	13	fat (gm):	2.2
cholesterol (mg):	42	sodium (mg):	321

CREOLE-STYLE LAMB SOUP

Makes 6 to 7 Servings.

1 large onion, finely chopped
2 large garlic cloves, minced
1 large sweet green pepper, diced
1 large celery stalk, diced
1 cup zucchini, diced
2 15-oz. cans reduced-sodium tomato sauce, *or* regular tomato sauce
1 cup water
3 cups beef stock (pg. 199), *or* broth (defatted)
1 lb. lean stewing lamb, trimmed of all fat and cut into ½-in. cubes (or use lamb leg or loin cubes)
⅓ cup fresh parsley leaves, chopped
⅓ cup uncooked white rice
1 bay leaf
Dash cayenne pepper
2 teaspoons sugar
1 teaspoon dried marjoram leaves
½ teaspoon dried thyme leaves
½ teaspoon dried basil leaves
¼ teaspoon powdered mustard
¼ teaspoon black pepper
Salt to taste

Combine all ingredients, except salt, in crock pot. Cover and cook on high setting 1 hour. Change setting to low and cook an additional 7 to 9 hours until meat and vegetables are tender and flavors are well blended. With large, shallow spoon, skim fat from top of soup and discard. Add salt if desired. Stir before serving.

Number of Servings: 7 (data per serving)

calories:	173	protein (gm):	14.7
% calories from fat:	27	fat (gm):	5.2
cholesterol (mg):	39	sodium (mg):	246

Easy Goulash Soup

Makes 6 to 8 Servings.

1 large onion, finely chopped
1 large carrot, thinly sliced
1 large celery stalk, diced
2 large garlic cloves, minced
2 cups potatoes, peeled and diced
1 cup ¾-in.-long fresh green bean pieces, *or*
   1 cup French-style frozen green beans
2 tablespoons pearl barley
1 lb. beef round, trimmed and cut into
   ¾-in. cubes
5 cups water
4 beef bouillon cubes
1 bay leaf
2 teaspoons sugar
1½ teaspoons paprika
½ teaspoon powdered mustard
½ teaspoon dried thyme
¼ teaspoon black pepper
1 15-oz. can reduced-sodium tomato sauce, *or*
   regular tomato sauce
2 tablespoons tomato paste
   Salt to taste

Combine onion, carrot, celery, garlic, potatoes, green beans, barley, beef, water, bouillon cubes, bay leaf, sugar, paprika, mustard, thyme, and pepper in crock pot. Cook on high setting 1 hour. Change setting to low and cook an additional 7 or 8 hours.

In medium-sized bowl, stir together tomato sauce and tomato paste until well combined. Add to mixture. Cook an additional 1 to 1½ hours on high setting. Taste soup. Add salt if desired. Stir before serving.

This soup keeps 4 to 5 days in refrigerator.

Number of Servings: 8 *(data per serving)*

calories:	153	protein (gm):	15.1
% calories from fat:	16	fat (gm):	2.7
cholesterol (mg):	33	sodium (mg):	514

EASY BARLEY AND GARBANZO SOUP

Makes 6 to 7 Servings.

1 smoked pork hock (about ½ lb.)
6 cups very hot tap water
3 beef bouillon cubes
⅓ cup pearl barley
1 15-oz. can reduced-sodium tomato sauce, *or* regular tomato sauce
1 celery stalk, finely chopped
1 large carrot, finely chopped
2 tablespoons instant minced onions
2 teaspoons sugar
¼ teaspoon ground celery seed
½ teaspoon powdered mustard
¼ teaspoon dried thyme
Dash cayenne pepper
¼ teaspoon black pepper, preferably freshly ground
2 cups cooked garbanzo beans, *or* 1 15-oz. can garbanzo beans, well drained
1 16-oz. can reduced-sodium cut green beans, well drained, *or* regular green beans
Salt to taste

Combine all ingredients except garbanzo beans, green beans, and salt, in crock pot. Cook on high setting 1 hour. Change setting to low and cook an additional 7 or 8 hours or until barley is tender. Remove and discard pork hock. Add garbanzos and green beans and salt if desired, and cook an additional ½ hour on high. With a large, shallow spoon, skim off and discard fat from top of soup. Stir before serving.

This soup keeps 3 to 4 days in refrigerator.

Number of Servings: 7 *(data per serving)*

calories:	215	protein (gm):	12.0
% calories from fat:	15	fat (gm):	3.6
cholesterol (mg):	16	sodium (mg):	426

WORKDAY BEAN SOUP

This easy, economical crock pot soup is designed to fit into the typical work schedule. The beans are put into the pot at night before going to bed. The next morning, the rest of the ingredients are added. Ten or 12 hours later, when the cook returns home from work, a savory soup is waiting.

Makes 5 to 6 Servings.

1¼ cups dry pinto or cranberry beans, sorted and washed

1 cup dry Great Northern beans, sorted and washed

1 medium-sized smoked pork hock (about ¾ lb.)

1 large onion, chopped

2 medium-sized celery stalks, coarsely chopped

1 medium-sized carrot, chopped

½ cup sweet red or green pepper, finely diced

5 cups hot water

4 beef bouillon cubes

1 small bay leaf

3 tablespoons ketchup

2 tablespoons sugar

1 tablespoon apple cider vinegar

1¼ teaspoons chili powder

¼ teaspoon dried thyme leaves

¼ teaspoon powdered mustard

¼ teaspoon ground allspice

¼ teaspoon black pepper

1 8-oz. can tomato sauce

Put beans in crock pot. Cover them with about 3 in. of hot tap water. Cover pot; turn setting to low and let beans soak and cook 8 to 10 hours.

Turn out beans into colander, discarding water. Return beans to pot, along with all remaining ingredients, except tomato sauce. Stir ingredients well. Cover the pot and cook on low 10 to 12 hours. Discard bay leaf and pork hock. Using a large, shallow spoon, skim off and discard fat from soup surface. Stir in tomato sauce. Turn setting to high and allow soup to reheat to piping hot.

Keeps, refrigerated, 2 or 3 days.

Number of Servings: 6 (data per serving)

calories:	235	protein (gm):	14.2
% calories from fat:	10	fat (gm):	2.6
cholesterol (mg):	14	sodium (mg):	943

CHICKEN GUMBO

Black-eyed peas, okra, and succotash, all Southern favorites, combine nicely in this nourishing gumbo.

Makes 5 to 6 Servings.

1 10-oz. package frozen black-eyed peas, rinsed under hot water and thoroughly drained
2 large onions, finely chopped
1 medium-sized pork hock (about ¾ lb.)
1 lb. boneless, skinless chicken breasts, all visible fat removed
2 large celery stalks, chopped
½ cup diced sweet red pepper (if unavailable, substitute sweet green pepper)
3 tablespoons long-grain white rice, uncooked
1 large bay leaf
1 10-oz. package frozen succotash, rinsed under hot water and thoroughly drained
1 cup frozen sliced okra, rinsed under cool water and thoroughly drained
4 cups chicken bouillon reconstituted from chicken bouillon cubes and hot water
1 15-oz. can tomatoes, including juice
2 tablespoons fresh parsley leaves, finely chopped (optional)
¼ teaspoon dried thyme leaves
¼ teaspoon black pepper

I n the order listed, put peas, onions, pork hock, chicken, celery, red pepper, rice, bay leaf, succotash, okra, and bouillon into crock pot. Cover pot and turn to high setting. Cook 30 minutes. Then continue cooking on high 3 hours longer, *or* reduce heat to low and continue cooking 7 hours longer.

Using a slotted spoon, remove chicken pieces from pot and set aside to cool. Discard pork hock and bay leaf. Stir juice from tomatoes into pot. Chop tomatoes and stir them into pot, along with parsley, thyme, and pepper. Continue cooking on low about 15 minutes longer until soup is heated to hot again.

When the chicken is cool enough to handle, cut it into bite-sized pieces. Stir chicken into gumbo and cook several minutes longer until very hot. If gumbo is too thick, thin with a little hot water before serving.

Keeps, refrigerated, up to 2 days.

Number of Servings: 6 *(data per serving)*

calories:	306	protein (gm):	30.2
% calories from fat:	15	fat (gm):	5.1
cholesterol (mg):	65	sodium (mg):	775

STOCKS

CHICKEN STOCK

Rich in flavor, this stock is far superior to commercial chicken broth or bouillon. It can be kept in the refrigerator 2 to 3 days and frozen for up to 6 months. It's not necessary to use expensive chicken parts in making the stock. Backs, wings, and necks are fine. In fact, these parts can be saved when you buy whole chickens and then stored in the freezer. If you don't have a pot large enough to make the whole recipe, it can easily be halved.

◆

Note that the amount of salt called for yields a stock that tastes about as salty as commercial chicken broth. Naturally, less can be used. If you are on a salt-free diet, omit the salt entirely.

Makes About 10 Cups.

7	lbs. (approximately) bony chicken parts such as backs, wings, and necks
16	cups water
4	medium-sized carrots, coarsely sliced
4	large celery stalks, coarsely sliced
5 to 6	fresh parsley sprigs
2	parsnips, *or* 2 small turnips, peeled and diced
2	large onions, coarsely chopped
2	bay leaves
½	teaspoon dried thyme leaves
2	teaspoons salt
½	teaspoon (generous) black pepper

In a large stock-pot, combine chicken, water, carrots, celery, parsley, parsnips, and onions. Bring to a boil over medium-high heat. Cover, lower heat, and simmer gently 1½ hours, skimming foam from top of stock frequently during first 20 to 30 minutes.

Add all remaining ingredients. With cover of pot slightly ajar, simmer stock over low heat an additional 1½ hours, stirring occasionally. Remove chicken and vegetables with slotted spoon. With large, shallow spoon, skim fat from top of stock and discard.

Strain stock through a strainer, and measure quantity. You should have about 10 cups of liquid. If more has evaporated, add a bit of water. If there is too much liquid, wash out pot in which stock was prepared. Return stock to pot and boil it down until only 10 or 11 cups remain.

For completely fat-free stock, refrigerate overnight. Then use a large, shallow spoon to lift off and discard solid fat.

Stock may be refrigerated 2 or 3 days and frozen for up to 6 months.

Number of 1-Cup Servings: 10 *(data per serving)*

calories:	30	protein (gm):	4.9
% calories from fat:	12	fat (gm):	0.4
cholesterol (mg):	1	sodium (mg):	426

VEGETABLE STOCK

*A nice base for vegetarian soups, this flavorful stock can be
substituted in many recipes that call for vegetable bouillon or
vegetable bouillon reconstituted from cubes or powder. However,
the homemade stock is not as concentrated as vegetable bouillon.
In general, use 2 cups of homemade vegetable stock for every
1 cup of vegetable bouillon and 1 cup of water.
Because this homemade stock has only a modest amount of salt,
you may need to increase the salt slightly in recipes using it.
Or if you are on a low-salt diet, you can omit the salt from
the stock entirely.
As vegetable stocks do not keep well, use the mixture within
24 hours if stored in the refrigerator. The stock can be frozen for
4 to 6 weeks. Also, the recipe can be doubled if desired.*

Makes 4 Cups.

1 tablespoon canola, safflower, or corn oil
2 large onions, finely chopped
1 large garlic clove, minced
1 large potato, well scrubbed and diced
3 large celery stalks, including leaves, thinly
  sliced
5 cups water, divided
1 large carrot, well scrubbed and thinly sliced
1 large turnip, well scrubbed, root and stem end
  removed, and diced
½ cup fresh parsley leaves, finely chopped
2 large bay leaves
¼ teaspoon black pepper
¾ teaspoon (scant) salt

In a large, heavy saucepan, combine oil, onion, garlic, potato, celery, and 3 tablespoons water. Over medium heat, cook vegetables about 10 minutes, being careful not to brown them. Stir frequently. If vegetables begin to brown, add a bit more water.

Add all remaining ingredients, and stir to mix well. Cover and bring to a boil over high heat. Lower heat and simmer stock about 1 hour.

Strain stock through a strainer, discarding vegetables. Measure stock. If there is less than 4 cups of liquid, add water as necessary to yield 4 cups With a large, flat spoon, skim oil from top of stock and discard.

Number of 1-Cup Servings: 4   (data per serving)

calories:	29	protein (gm):	1.7
% calories from fat:	19	fat (gm):	0.6
cholesterol (mg):	0	sodium (mg):	399

BEEF STOCK

This is a basic stock that can be employed whenever beef stock is called for in our recipes. Like our other stocks, this one is lightly salted. If you are on a salt-restricted diet, simply omit the salt from the recipe below.
Although this stock benefits from long simmering, it doesn't require much attention. Just make a quick check now and then to be sure it isn't boiling too hard.

Makes About 3 Quarts.

- 3 lbs. beef bones, preferably marrow bones sawed into 2-in. pieces
- 2 lbs. meaty beef plate ribs
- 4 large onions, coarsely chopped
- 2 large celery stalks, coarsely sliced
- 2 large carrots, coarsely sliced
- 2 medium-sized turnips, very coarsely chopped
- 14 cups water, divided
- ⅓ cup fresh parsley, chopped
- 3 bay leaves
- 1 teaspoon black peppercorns
- ½ teaspoon dried thyme leaves
- 2 whole cloves
- 2½ teaspoons salt

Preheat oven to 400 degrees. Rinse and drain marrow bones and plate ribs well. Pat them dry with paper towels. Spread out bones, ribs, onions, celery, carrots, and turnips in very large roasting pan (or use two smaller ones). Roast mixture 1⅓ to 1½ hours, stirring occasionally to ensure even browning and to prevent burning.

Transfer contents of roasting pan to large soup pot or a stock-pot. Put 2 cups water into roasting pan. Using a wooden spoon, scrape up any browned bits sticking to bottom. Transfer water and browned bits to stock-pot. Add remaining 12 cups water and parsley. Bring mixture to a boil over high heat. Cover pot and adjust heat so mixture gently simmers 1 hour.

Skim any scum from broth surface. Add remaining ingredients and continue simmering, covered, at least 2½ hours and up to 6 hours longer

Remove pot from heat. Strain stock through fine sieve, discarding bones and vegetables. If stock must be used immediately, very carefully skim off and discard fat from surface, using large, shallow spoon. (If time permits, refrigerate stock until fat solidifies and then lift it off.)

This stock may be refrigerated up to 4 days or frozen for several months.

Number of 1-Cup Servings: 12 (data per serving)

calories:	16	protein (gm):	2.7
% calories from fat:	28	fat (gm):	0.5
cholesterol (mg):	0	sodium (mg):	444

FISH STOCK

Of all stocks, fish stock is the easiest and most economical to prepare. Fresh fish frames (skeletons) can usually be obtained free or for a small charge from seafood markets and fishmongers. And the ingredients need only simmer about a half-hour to yield good, rich stock.
Be sure to use only very fresh, clean, non-oily white fish. Frames from darker-fleshed varieties make stock too strong. Also, avoid preparing fish stock in an aluminum pot, as the metal may react and lend a metallic taste to the stock or discolor it.

Makes About 2 Quarts.

4¼	lbs. frames and heads from flounder, sole, haddock, etc.
8	cups water
½	cup dry white wine
1	medium-sized onion, coarsely chopped
1	small celery stalk, coarsely sliced
1	small carrot, coarsely sliced
7 or 8	fresh parsley sprigs
1	small bay leaf
1½	teaspoons fresh lemon juice
½	teaspoon black peppercorns
⅛	teaspoon dried thyme leaves
1¼	teaspoons salt

Thoroughly rinse fish frames and drain them. Rinse heads, being careful to wash away blood. (If they seem bloody, soak in cold water a few minutes. Then drain and rinse heads well and place in water again. Repeat until water stays clear.)

Combine frames and heads in 6-quart or larger pot, along with all remaining ingredients, except salt. Bring to a boil over medium heat. Cover and lower heat; simmer about 30 minutes.

Strain stock through a fine sieve, discarding frames and vegetables. Stir in salt.

This stock may be refrigerated up to 3 days or frozen for several months.

Number of 1-Cup Servings: 8   *(data per serving)*

calories:	39	protein (gm):	5.3
% calories from fat:	0	fat (gm):	0.0
cholesterol (mg):	0	sodium (mg):	333

INDEX